MEDICAL USE OF MARIJUANA:
POLICY, REGULATORY AND LEGAL ISSUES

MEDICAL USE OF MARIJUANA: POLICY, REGULATORY AND LEGAL ISSUES

TATIANA SHOHOV (EDITOR)

Nova Science Publishers, Inc.
New York

Senior Editors: Susan Boriotti and Donna Dennis
Office Manager: Annette Hellinger
Graphics: Wanda Serrano
Editorial Production: Maya Columbus, Vladimir Klestov,
Matthew Kozlowski and Tom Moceri
Circulation: Ave Maria Gonzalez, Vera Popovic, Luis Aviles, Raymond Davis,
Melissa Diaz, Magdalena Nunez, Marlene Nunez and Jeannie Pappas
Communications and Acquisitions: Serge P. Shohov
Marketing: Cathy DeGregory

Library of Congress Cataloging-in-Publication Data
Available Upon Request

ISBN: 1-59033-754-9.

Copyright © 2003 by Nova Science Publishers, Inc.
400 Oser Ave, Suite 1600
Hauppauge, New York 11788-3619
Tele. 631-231-7269   Fax 631-231-8175
e-mail: Novascience@earthlink.net
Web Site: http://www.novapublishers.com

Printed in the United States of America

CONTENTS

PREFACE

In recent years, there has been much debate over whether marijuana, an illegal drug, can provide patients with a level of therapeutic relief comparable to existing pharmaceutical treatments. While this idea is hardly new, it is advanced by some proponents as deserving more scientific inquiry. Advocates for the medical use of marijuana contend that there is already sufficient scientific evidence to justify rescheduling marijuana under the Controlled Substances Act, a change that would give it the necessary legal recognition to be used for medicinal purposes. This has already occurred in the case of dronabinol, the synthetic form of the main psychoactive ingredient in marijuana, which has been available as an oral prescription drug since 1986 under its brand name Marinol.

To address these viewpoints, several comprehensive studies were done in the late 1990s to evaluate medicinal claims made for smoked marijuana and determine whether they are supported by convincing scientific evidence. In 1997, the NIH convened an Ad Hoc Group of Experts, which concluded that scientific evidence was insufficient to definitively assess marijuana's therapeutic potential and advised that the traditional scientific process should be allowed to evaluate the drug's use for certain disorders. In its 1999 report *Marijuana and Medicine. Assessing the Science Base*, the Institute of Medicine (IOM) concluded that the therapeutic effects of smoking marijuana were modest. IOM noted, however, that while marijuana's active components are potentially effective in treating certain medical conditions, they should be tested rigorously in controlled clinical trials.

The medical marijuana debate gained attention at the state level in 1996, when voters in California and Arizona approved ballot initiatives allowing doctors to prescribe the drug for therapeutic uses. In 1998, similar propositions were adopted in Alaska, Nevada, Oregon, and Washington, and reaffirmed in Arizona. Voters in Maine adopted a medical marijuana initiative in 1999. In 2000, medical marijuana was approved by voters in Colorado, reconfirmed in Nevada, and passed by the legislature in Hawaii. Federal health officials assert that these initiatives are part of a strategy to soften the nation's drug laws, and that public policy would be better served if science, rather than the ballot box, were used to judge the drug's utility.

Congress has responded to the state initiatives by passing various measures reconfirming marijuana's status as a Schedule I controlled substance with no currently accepted medical use in the United States. Congress has also said that it supports the existing federal legal process for determining the safety and effectiveness of drugs, and opposes efforts to circumvent this process by legalizing marijuana, or any other Schedule I controlled drug, for medical use without valid clinical evidence and the approval of the Food and Drug Administration. Although bills have been introduced in Congress to let doctors prescribe marijuana in states with laws that allow it, thus far Congress has opposed this idea until the drug's alleged therapeutic benefits have been confirmed scientifically. Until such studies are done, and more convincing data emerge, reports of marijuana's medicinal prowess will hinge as much on anecdotal evidence as the controlled clinical investigation.

This book assesses the current issues and examines the controversies regarding the marijuana legalization issue.

Chapter 1

MARIJUANA: BACKGROUND, FACTS AND DIFFERENT VIEWS[*]

Tatiana Shohov (Editor)

INTRODUCTION

Marijuana is the most commonly used illicit drug in the United States. A dry, shredded green/brown mix of flowers, stems, seeds, and leaves of the hemp plant Cannabis sativa, it usually is smoked as a cigarette (joint), or in a pipe (bong). It also is smoked in blunts, which are cigars that have been emptied of tobacco and refilled with marijuana, often in combination with another drug. Use also might include mixing marijuana in food or brewing it as a tea. As a more concentrated, resinous form it is called hashish and, as a sticky black liquid, hash oil. Marijuana smoke has a pungent and distinctive, usually sweet-and-sour odor. There are countless street terms for marijuana including pot, herb, weed, grass, widow, ganja, and hash, as well as terms derived from trademarked varieties of cannabis, such as Bubble Gum®, Northern Lights®, Juicy Fruit®, Afghani #1®, and a number of Skunk varieties.

The main active chemical in marijuana is THC (delta-9-tetrahydrocannabinol). The membranes of certain nerve cells in the brain contain protein receptors that bind to THC. Once securely in place, THC kicks off a series

---

[*] This chapter contains information excerpted from several different websites including: http://www.compassionateaccess.org, http://www.mpp.org and http://www.nida.nih.gov.

of cellular reactions that ultimately lead to the high that users experience when they smoke marijuana.

EXTENT OF USE

In 2001, over 12 million Americans age 12 and older used marijuana at least once in the month prior to being surveyed. That is more than three quarters (76 percent) of the total number of Americans who used any illicit drug in the past month in 2001. Of the 76 percent, more than half (56 percent) consumed only marijuana; 20 percent used marijuana and another illicit drug; and the remaining 24 percent used an illicit drug or drugs other than marijuana.[1]

Although marijuana is the most commonly used illicit drug in the United States, among students in the 8th, 10th, and 12th grades nationwide its use remained stable from 1999 through 2001.[2] Among 8th graders, however, past year use has decreased, from 18.3 percent in 1996 to 15.4 percent in 2001. Also in 2001, more than half (57.4 percent) of 12th graders believed it was harmful to smoke marijuana regularly and 79.3 percent disapproved of regular marijuana use. Since 1975, 83 percent to 90 percent of every 12th grade class surveyed has found it "fairly easy" or "very easy" to obtain marijuana.[3]

Data for drug-related hospital emergency department visits in the continental United States recently showed a 15 percent increase in the number of visits to an emergency room that were induced by or related to the use of marijuana (referred to as mentions), from 96,426 in 2000 to 110,512 in 2001. The 12 to 34 age range was involved most frequently in these mentions. For emergency room patients in the 12 to 17 age range, the rate of marijuana mentions increased 23 percent between 1999 and 2001 (from 55 to 68 per 100,000 population) and 126 percent (from 30 to 68 per 100,000 population) since 1994.[4]

---

[1] These data are from the annual National Household Survey on Drug Abuse, funded by the Substance Abuse and Mental Health Services Administration, U.S. Department of Health and Human Services (DHHS). The latest data (2001) are available at 1-800-729-6686 or online at www.samhsa.gov.

[2] These data are from the Monitoring the Future Survey, funded by National Institute on Drug Abuse, National Institutes of Health, DHHS, and conducted by the University of Michigan's Institute for Social Research. The survey has tracked 12th graders' illicit drug use and related attitudes since 1975; in 1991, 8th and 10th graders were added to the study. The latest data (2001) are online at www.drugabuse.gov.

[3] Ibid.

[4] These data are from the annual Drug Abuse Warning Network, funded by the Substance Abuse and Mental Health Services Administration, DHHS. The survey provides information about emergency department visits that are induced by or related to the use of an illicit drug or the

EFFECTS ON THE BRAIN

Scientists have learned a great deal about how THC acts in the brain to produce its many effects. When someone smokes marijuana, THC rapidly passes from the lungs into the bloodstream, which carries the chemical to organs throughout the body, including the brain.

In the brain, THC connects to specific sites called cannabinoid receptors on nerve cells and influences the activity of those cells. Some brain areas have many cannabinoid receptors; others have few or none. Many cannabinoid receptors are found in the parts of the brain that influence pleasure, memory, thought, concentration, sensory and time perception, and coordinated movement.[5]

The short-term effects of marijuana use can include problems with memory and learning; distorted perception; difficulty in thinking and problem solving; loss of coordination; and increased heart rate. Research findings for long-term marijuana use indicate some changes in the brain similar to those seen after long-term use of other major drugs of abuse. For example, cannabinoid (THC or synthetic forms of THC) withdrawal in chronically exposed animals leads to an increase in the activation of the stress-response system[6] and changes in the activity of nerve cells containing dopamine.[7] Dopamine neurons are involved in the regulation of motivation and reward, and are directly or indirectly affected by all drugs of abuse.

EFFECTS ON THE HEART

One study has indicated that a user's risk of heart attack more than quadruples in the first hour after smoking marijuana.[8] The researchers suggest that such an effect might occur from marijuana's effects on blood pressure and heart rate and reduced oxygen-carrying capacity of blood.

---

nonmedical use of a legal drug. The latest data (2001) are available at 1-800-729-6686 or online at www.samhsa.gov.

[5] Herkenham M, Lynn A., Little MD, Johnson MR, et al: Cannabinoid receptor localization in the brain. Proc Natl Acad Sci, USA 87:1932-1936, 1990.

[6] Rodriguez de Fonseca F, et al: Activation of cortocotropin-releasing factor in the limbic system during cannabinoid withdrawal. Science 276(5321):2050-2064, 1997.

[7] Diana M, Melis M, Muntoni AL, et al: Mesolimbic dopaminergic decline after cannabinoid withdrawal. Proc. Natl. Acad. Sci 95:10269-10273, 1998.

[8] Mittleman MA, Lewis RA, Maclure M, et al: Triggering myocardial infarction by marijuana. Circulation 103:2805-2809, 2001.

EFFECTS ON THE LUNGS

A study of 450 individuals found that people who smoke marijuana frequently but do not smoke tobacco have more health problems and miss more days of work than nonsmokers.[9] Many of the extra sick days among the marijuana smokers in the study were for respiratory illnesses.

Even infrequent use can cause burning and stinging of the mouth and throat, often accompanied by a heavy cough. Someone who smokes marijuana regularly may have many of the same respiratory problems that tobacco smokers do, such as daily cough and phlegm production, more frequent acute chest illness, a heightened risk of lung infections, and a greater tendency to obstructed airways.[10]

Cancer of the respiratory tract and lungs may also be promoted by marijuana smoke.[11] A study comparing 173 cancer patients and 176 healthy individuals produced strong evidence that smoking marijuana increases the likelihood of developing cancer of the head or neck, and the more marijuana smoked the greater the increase.[12] A statistical analysis of the data suggested that marijuana smoking doubled or tripled the risk of these cancers.

Marijuana use has the potential to promote cancer of the lungs and other parts of the respiratory tract because it contains irritants and carcinogens.[13] In fact, marijuana smoke contains 50 to 70 percent more carcinogenic hydrocarbons than does tobacco smoke.[14] It also produces high levels of an enzyme that converts certain hydrocarbons into their carcinogenic form—levels that may accelerate the changes that ultimately produce malignant cells.[15] Marijuana users usually inhale more deeply and hold their breath longer than tobacco smokers do, which increases the lungs' exposure to carcinogenic smoke. These facts suggest that, puff for puff, smoking marijuana may increase the risk of cancer more than smoking tobacco.

---

[9] Polen M R, Sidney S, Tekawa IS, et al: Health care use by frequent marijuana smokers who do not smoke tobacco. West J Med 158:596-601, 1993.

[10] Tashkin DP: Pulmonary complications of smoked substance abuse. West J Med 152:525-530, 1990.

[11] Ibid.

[12] Zhang ZF, Morgenstern H, Spitz MR, et al: Marijuana use and increased risk of squamous cell carcinoma of the head and neck. Cancer Epidemiology, Biomarkers & Prevention 6:1071-1078, 1999.

[13] Sridhar KS, Raub WA, Weatherby, NL Jr, et al: Possible role of marijuana smoking as a carcinogen in the development of lung cancer at a young age. Journal of Psychoactive Drugs 26(3):285-288, 1994.

[14] Hoffman D, Brunnemann KD, Gori GB, et al: On the carcinogenicity of marijuana smoke. In: VC Runeckles, ed, Recent Advances in Phytochemistry. New York. Plenum, 1975.

[15] Cohen S: Adverse effects of marijuana: selected issues. Annals of the New York Academy of Sciences 362:119-124, 1981.

OTHER HEALTH EFFECTS

Some of marijuana's adverse health effects may occur because THC impairs the immune system's ability to fight off infectious diseases and cancer. In laboratory experiments that exposed animal and human cells to THC or other marijuana ingredients, the normal disease-preventing reactions of many of the key types of immune cells were inhibited.[16] In other studies, mice exposed to THC or related substances were more likely than unexposed mice to develop bacterial infections and tumors.[17, 18]

EFFECTS OF HEAVY MARIJUANA USE ON LEARNING AND SOCIAL BEHAVIOR

Depression,[19] anxiety,[20] and personality disturbances[21] are all associated with marijuana use. Research clearly demonstrates that marijuana use has potential to cause problems in daily life or make a person's existing problems worse. Because marijuana compromises the ability to learn and remember information, the more a person uses marijuana the more he or she is likely to fall behind in accumulating intellectual, job, or social skills. Moreover, research has shown that marijuana's adverse impact on memory and learning can last for days or weeks after the acute effects of the drug wear off.[22, 23]

Students who smoke marijuana get lower grades and are less likely to graduate from high school, compared to their non-smoking peers.[24, 25, 26, 27] In one

---

[16] Adams IB, Martin BR: Cannabis: pharmacology and toxicology in animals and humans. Addiction 91:1585-1614, 1996.

[17] Klein TW, Newton C, Friedman H: Resistance to Legionella pneumophila suppressed by the marijuana component, tetrahydrocannabinol. J Infectious Disease 169:1177-1179, 1994.

[18] Zhu L, Stolina M, Sharma S, et al: Delta-9 tetrahydrocannabinol inhibits antitumor immunity by a CB2 receptor-mediated, cytokine-dependent pathway. J Immunology, 2000, pp. 373-380.

[19] Brook JS, et al: The effect of early marijuana use on later anxiety and depressive symptoms. NYS Psychologist, January 2001, pp. 35-39.

[20] Green BE, Ritter C: Marijuana use and depression. J Health Soc Behav 41(1):40-49, 2000.

[21] Brook JS, Cohen P, Brook DW: Longitudinal study of co-occurring psychiatric disorders and substance use. J Acad Child and Adolescent Psych 37:322-330, 1998.

[22] Pope HG, Yurgelun-Todd D: The residual cognitive effects of heavy marijuana use in college students. JAMA 272(7):521-527, 1996.

[23] Block RI, Ghoneim MM: Effects of chronic marijuana use on human cognition. Psychopharmacology 100(1-2):219-228, 1993.

[24] Lynskey M, Hall W: The effects of adolescent cannabis use on educational attainment: a review. Addiction 95(11):1621-1630, 2000.

study, researchers compared marijuana-smoking and non-smoking 12th-graders' scores on standardized tests of verbal and mathematical skills. Although all of the students had scored equally well in 4th grade, the marijuana smokers' scores were significantly lower in 12th grade.[28]

A study of 129 college students found that, for heavy users of marijuana (those who smoked the drug at least 27 of the preceding 30 days), critical skills related to attention, memory, and learning were significantly impaired even after they had not used the drug for at least 24 hours.[29] The heavy marijuana users in the study had more trouble sustaining and shifting their attention and in registering, organizing, and using information than did the study participants who had used marijuana no more than 3 of the previous 30 days. As a result, someone who smokes marijuana once daily may be functioning at a reduced intellectual level all of the time.

More recently, the same researchers showed that the ability of a group of long-term heavy marijuana users to recall words from a list remained impaired for a week after quitting, but returned to normal within 4 weeks.[30] An implication of this finding is that some cognitive abilities may be restored in individuals who quit smoking marijuana, even after long-term heavy use.

Workers who smoke marijuana are more likely than their coworkers to have problems on the job. Several studies associate workers' marijuana smoking with increased absences, tardiness, accidents, workers' compensation claims, and job turnover. A study of municipal workers found that those who used marijuana on or off the job reported more "withdrawal behaviors"—such as leaving work without permission, daydreaming, spending work time on personal matters, and shirking tasks—that adversely affect productivity and morale.[31]

[25] Kandel DB, Davies M: High school students who use crack and other drugs. Arch Gen Psychiatry 53(1):71-80, 1996.

[26] Rob M, Reynolds I, Finlayson PF: Adolescent marijuana use: risk factors and implications. Aust NZ J Psychiatry 24(1):45-56, 1990.

[27] Brook JS, Balka EB, Whiteman M: The risks for late adolescence of early adolescent marijuana use. Am J Public Health 89(10):1549-1554, 1999.

[28] Block RI, Ghoneim MM: Effects of chronic marijuana use on human cognition. Psychopharmacology 100(1-2):219 228, 1993.

[29] Ibid ref 22.

[30] Pope, Gruber, Hudson, et al: Neuropsychological performance in long-term cannabis users. Archives of General Psychiatry.

[31] Lehman WE, Simpson DD: Employee substance abuse and on-the-job behaviors. Journal of Applied Psychology 77(3):309-321, 1992.

EFFECTS ON PREGNANCY

Research has shown that babies born to women who used marijuana during their pregnancies display altered responses to visual stimuli, increased tremulousness, and a high-pitched cry, which may indicate problems with neurological development.[32] During infancy and preschool years, marijuana-exposed children have been observed to have more behavioral problems and poorer performance on tasks of visual perception, language comprehension, sustained attention, and memory.[33, 34] In school, these children are more likely to exhibit deficits in decision-making skills, memory, and the ability to remain attentive.[35, 36, 37]

ADDICTIVE POTENTIAL

Long-term marijuana use can lead to psychological addiction for some people. Drug craving can make it hard for long-term marijuana smokers to stop using the drug. People trying to quit report irritability, sleeplessness, and anxiety.[38] They also display increased aggression on psychological tests, peaking approximately one week after the last use of the drug.[39]

GENETIC VULNERABILITY

Scientists have found that whether an individual has positive or negative sensations after smoking marijuana can be influenced by heredity. A 1997 study[40] demonstrated that identical male twins were more likely than non-identical male

---

[32] Lester, BM; Dreher, M: Effects of marijuana use during pregnancy on newborn cry. Child Development 60:764-771, 1989.

[33] Fried, PA: The Ottawa prenatal prospective study (OPPS): methodological issues and findings— it's easy to throw the baby out with the bath water. Life Sciences 56:2159-2168, 1995.

[34] Fried, PA: Prenatal exposure to marihuana and tobacco during infancy, early and middle childhood: effects and an attempt at synthesis. Arch Toxicol Supp 17:233-60, 1995.

[35] Ibid ref 33.

[36] Ibid ref 34.

[37] Cornelius MD, Taylor PM, Geva D, et al: Prenatal tobacco and marijuana use among adolescents: effects on offspring gestational age, growth, and morphology. Pediatrics 95:738-743, 1995.

[38] Kouri EM, Pope HG, Lukas SE: Changes in aggressive behavior during withdrawal from long-term marijuana use. Psychopharmacology 143:302-308, 1999.

[39] Haney M, Ward AS, Comer SD, et al: Abstinence symptoms following smoked marijuana in humans. Psychopharmacology 141:395-404, 1999.

[40] Lyons MJ, et al: Addiction 92(4):409-417, 1997.

twins to report similar responses to marijuana use, indicating a genetic basis for their response to the drug. (Identical twins share all of their genes.)

It also was discovered that the twins' shared or family environment before age 18 had no detectable influence on their response to marijuana. Certain environmental factors, however, such as the availability of marijuana, expectations about how the drug would affect them, the influence of friends and social contacts, and other factors that differentiate experiences of identical twins were found to have an important effect.

TREATING MARIJUANA PROBLEMS

The latest treatment data indicate that, in 1999, marijuana was the primary drug of abuse in about 14 percent (223,597) of all admissions to treatment facilities in the United States. Marijuana admissions were primarily male (77 percent), white (58 percent), and young (47 percent under 20 years old). Those in treatment for primary marijuana use had begun use at an early age; 57 percent had used it by age 14 and 92 percent had used it by 18.[41]

One study of adult marijuana users found comparable benefits from a 14-session cognitive-behavioral group treatment and a 2-session individual treatment that included motivational interviewing and advice on ways to reduce marijuana use. Participants were mostly men in their early thirties who had smoked marijuana daily for more than 10 years. By increasing patients' awareness of what triggers their marijuana use, both treatments sought to help patients devise avoidance strategies. Use, dependence symptoms, and psychosocial problems decreased for at least 1 year following both treatments; about 30 percent of users were abstinent during the last 3-month followup period.[42]

Another study suggests that giving patients vouchers that they can redeem for goods—such as movie passes, sporting equipment, or vocational training—may further improve outcomes.[43]

---

[41] These data from the Treatment Episode Data Set (TEDS) 1994-1999: National Admissions to Substance Abuse Treatment Services, November 2001, funded by the Substance Abuse and Mental Health Service Administration, DHHS. The latest data are available at 1-800-729-6686 or online at www.samhsa.gov.

[42] Stephens RS, Roffman RA, Curtin L: Comparison of extended versus brief treatments for marijuana use. J Consult Clin Psychol 68(5):898-908, 2000.

[43] Budney AJ, Higgins ST, Radonovich KJ, et al: Adding voucher-based incentives to coping skills and motivational enhancement improves outcomes during treatment for marijuana dependence. J Consult Clin Psychol 68(6):1051-1061, 2000.

Although no medications are currently available for treating marijuana abuse, recent discoveries about the workings of the THC receptors have raised the possibility of eventually developing a medication that will block the intoxicating effects of THC. Such a medication might be used to prevent relapse to marijuana abuse by lessening or eliminating its appeal.

Percentage of 8th-Graders Who Have Used Marijuana: Monitoring the Future Study, 2001

	1992	1993	1994	1995	1996	1997	1998	1999	2000	2001
Ever Used	11.2%	12.6%	16.7%	19.9%	23.1%	22.6%	22.2%	22.0%	20.3%	20.4%
Used in Past Year	7.2	9.2	13.0	15.8	18.3	17.7	16.9	16.5	15.6	15.4
Used in Past Month	3.7	5.1	7.8	9.1	11.3	10.2	9.7	9.7	9.1	9.2
Daily Use in Past Month	0.2	0.4	0.7	0.8	1.5	1.1	1.1	1.4	1.3	1.3

Percentage of 10th-Graders Who Have Used Marijuana: Monitoring the Future Study, 2001

	1992	1993	1994	1995	1996	1997	1998	1999	2000	2001
Ever Used	21.4%	24.4%	30.4%	34.1%	39.8%	42.3%	39.6%	40.9%	40.3%	40.1%
Used in Past Year	15.2	19.2	25.2	28.7	33.6	34.8	31.1	32.1	32.2	32.7
Used in Past Month	8.1	10.9	15.8	17.2	20.4	20.5	18.7	19.4	19.7	19.8
Daily Use in Past Month	0.8	1.0	2.2	2.8	3.5	3.7	3.6	3.8	3.8	4.5

Percentage of 12th-Graders Who Have Used Marijuana:
Monitoring the Future Study, 2001

	1979	1985	1991	1992	1993	1994	1995
Ever Used	60.4%	54.2%	36.7%	32.6%	35.3%	38.2%	41.7%
Used in Past Year	50.8	40.6	23.9	21.9	26.0	30.7	34.7
Used in Past Month	36.5	25.7	13.8	11.9	15.5	19.0	21.2
Daily Use in Past Month	10.3	4.9	2.0	1.9	2.4	3.6	4.6
	1995	1996	1997	1998	1999	2000	2001
Ever Used	41.7%	44.9%	49.6%	49.1%	49.7%	48.8%	49.0%
Used in Past Year	34.7	35.8	38.5	37.5	37.8	36.5	37.0
Used in Past Month	21.2	21.9	23.7	22.8	23.1	21.6	22.4
Daily Use in Past Month	4.6	4.9	5.8	5.6	6.0	6.0	5.8

These data are from the 2001 Monitoring the Future (MTF) Survey, funded by National Institute on Drug Abuse, National Institutes of Health, DHHS, and conducted by the University of Michigan's Institute for Social Research. The survey has tracked 12th graders' illicit drug use and related attitudes since 1975; in 1991, 8th and 10th graders were added to the study. The latest data (2001) are online at www.drugabuse.gov.

COALITION FOR COMPASSIONATE ACCESS

The Coalition for Compassionate Access placed a full-page ad in the Wednesday, March 6, edition of *The New York Times* (page A9), calling on the Bush administration to implement the recommendation of the National Academy of Sciences that -- in its landmark 1999 report -- urged the federal government to give seriously ill people immediate legal access to medical marijuana on a case-by-case basis.

The White House drug czar's office used $1 million of taxpayer money to commission the NAS report, yet the federal government has refused to implement its recommendations for the past three years.

In the coming months, the Coalition for Compassionate Access will continue to grow as additional state legislators, clergy, celebrities, and organizations add their names to the sign-on letter.

More advertising and other media outreach efforts are being planned. Eventually, the pressure will be so great that the Bush administration will find it easier to change federal policy, rather than being accused of ignoring the science that supports marijuana's therapeutic value, as well as the 73% of the American people who support making marijuana medically available.

The only question is this: How long will the Bush administration stall before it finally follows the recommendation of the National Academy of Sciences?

For thousands of years, marijuana has been used to treat a wide variety of ailments. Until 1937, marijuana *(Cannabis sativa L.)* was legal in the United States for all purposes. Presently, federal law allows only seven (7) Americans to use marijuana as a medicine.

On March 17, 1999, the National Academy of Sciences' Institute of Medicine (IOM) concluded that "there are some limited circumstances in which we recommend smoking marijuana for medical uses." The IOM report released that day was the result of two years of research that was funded by the White House drug policy office, which comprised a metaanalysis of all existing data on marijuana's therapeutic uses.

MEDICINAL VALUE

Scientific evidence verifies that marijuana has the following therapeutic effects:

- Relief from nausea and increase of appetite;
- Reduction of intraocular ("within the eye") pressure;
- Reduction of muscle spasms;
- Relief from chronic pain.

Consequently, it is sometimes used to treat the symptoms of AIDS, cancer, multiple sclerosis, and other serious conditions. Nevertheless, federal laws and the laws of most states leave these patients subject to arrests, fines, court costs, property forfeiture, incarceration, probation, and criminal records.

FEDERAL LAW

The Marijuana Tax Act of 1937 federally prohibited marijuana. Dr. William C. Woodward of the American Medical Association opposed the Act, testifying that prohibition would ultimately prevent the medicinal uses of marijuana. The Controlled Substances Act of 1970 placed all illicit and prescription drugs into five "schedules" (categories). Marijuana was placed in Schedule I, defining the substance as having a high potential for abuse, no currently accepted medicinal use in treatment in the United States, and a lack of accepted safety for use under medical supervision. The federal penalty for possessing even one marijuana cigarette is up to a year in prison.

THE STRUGGLE IN COURT

In 1972, a petition was submitted to the Bureau of Narcotics and Dangerous Drugs—now the Drug Enforcement Administration (DEA)—to reschedule marijuana to make it available by prescription. After 16 years of court battles, the DEA's chief administrative law judge, Francis L. Young, ruled:

> "Marijuana, in its natural form, is one of the safest therapeutically active substances known. ...
> "... [T]he provisions of the [Controlled Substances] Act permit and require the transfer of marijuana from Schedule I to Schedule II.
> "It would be unreasonable, arbitrary and capricious for DEA to continue to stand between those sufferers and the benefits of this substance. ..."
> (September 6, 1988)

Marijuana's placement in Schedule II would enable doctors to prescribe it to their patients. **But top DEA officials rejected Judge Young's ruling and refused to reschedule marijuana.** Two appeals later, petitioners experienced their first defeat in the 22-year-old lawsuit. On February 18, 1994, the U.S. Court of Appeals (D.C. Circuit) ruled that the DEA is allowed to reject its judge's ruling and set its own criteria—enabling the DEA to keep marijuana in Schedule I.

TEMPORARY COMPASSION

In 1975, Robert Randall, who suffered from glaucoma, was arrested for cultivating his own marijuana. He won his case by using the "medical necessity defense," forcing the government to find a way to provide him with his medicine. As a result, the Investigational New Drug (IND) compassionate access program was established, allowing patients to apply for special permission to receive marijuana from the federal government.

In 1992, the U.S. Public Health Service closed the program to all new applicants. On December 1, 1999, the U.S. Department of Health and Human Services implemented its medical marijuana policy restating that the IND program would not be reopened. Consequently, the IND program remains in operation only for the seven surviving previously approved patients.

PUBLIC OPINION

There is tremendous public support for allowing patients to use medical marijuana:

- Since 1996, a majority of voters in Alaska, Arizona, California, Colorado, the District of Columbia, Maine, Nevada, Oregon, and Washington state have voted in favor of ballot initiatives to remove criminal penalties for seriously ill people who grow or possess medical marijuana.

- A 1990 scientific survey of oncologists (cancer specialists) found that 54% of those with an opinion favored the controlled medical availability of marijuana and 44% had already broken the law by suggesting at least once that a patient obtain marijuana illegally. [R.Doblin& M.Kleiman, "Marijuana as Antiemetic Medicine," *Journal of Clinical Oncology 9* (1991): 1314-1319.]

- A Pew Research poll conducted September 14-19, 2001, found that 73% of American adults supported permitting doctors to prescribe marijuana for their patients. All other public opinion polls taken since the 1990s have shown between 60% and 80% support for making marijuana medically available.

MARIJUANA POLICY PROJECT

With 12,000 members nationwide, the Marijuana Policy Project (MPP) is the largest marijuana policy reform organization in the United States. MPP works to minimize the harm associated with marijuana -- both the consumption of marijuana and the laws that are intended to prohibit such use. MPP believes that the greatest harm associated with marijuana is imprisonment. To this end, MPP focuses on removing criminal penalties for marijuana use, with a particular emphasis on making marijuana medically available to seriously ill people who have the approval of their doctors.

MPP MISSION STATEMENT

In the United States, more than 70 million people have tried marijuana, and millions of adults still consume it on a regular basis. Almost everyone has a friend, relative, neighbor, or co-worker who consumes marijuana. Because of the widespread economic and criminal justice ramifications of the illicit marijuana market and of Marijuana Prohibition, the marijuana phenomenon touches nearly everyone's life.

All drugs are potentially harmful; marijuana is no exception -- and the entire range of marijuana policies, from total prohibition to total legalization, has drawbacks as well as benefits. As with alcohol and tobacco, there is no simple solution.

The Marijuana Policy Project (MPP) understands that no one policy will solve all problems. Each potentially harmful effect of marijuana consumption and the myriad public and private marijuana control efforts must be thoroughly evaluated. Each policy option should be judged according to whether the overall harm is reduced or increased. Furthermore, public policies must be grounded in the reality that marijuana consumption is already widespread despite the present prohibition laws.

A "marijuana-free America" has been proven to be an unrealistic goal.

Prohibition: Turning a Problem into a Disaster

Marijuana prohibition simply does not work. More than 70 million Americans have tried marijuana, and millions of adults consume it on a regular basis. Present marijuana policies do not prevent people from using marijuana -- instead, they punish those who are unlucky enough to get caught.

Marijuana prohibition creates a mixed drug market, which puts marijuana consumers in contact with hard-drug dealers. **Regulating marijuana sales -- and allowing adults to grow their own -- would separate marijuana from cocaine, heroin, and other hard drugs.**

This approach works in Holland.

Banned Medicine

Marijuana is beneficial to people suffering from cancer, AIDS, glaucoma, multiple sclerosis, epilepsy, and chronic pain. Yet **only eight people** in the United States are currently allowed to use marijuana as medicine.

Millions of patients who could benefit from marijuana must **either suffer or use it illegally and risk arrest.**

Learning from History

Earlier this century, alcohol prohibition caused an increase in crime and violence, but it did not prevent people from drinking. Alcohol prohibition failed -- and was repealed in 1933.

Marijuana prohibition has also failed. In 1972, President Nixon's National Commission on Marijuana and Drug Abuse declared that adults should not be criminalized for using marijuana.

Nixon ignored his advisors and escalated his "war on drugs." By the end of the decade, marijuana use and abuse had increased manyfold.

A "marijuana-free America" has proven to be an unrealistic goal. And by wasting valuable law-enforcement resources and maintaining an unregulated market, prohibition only makes matters worse for marijuana consumers and society as a whole.

Policies should instead minimize the harm associated with marijuana.

Other Damaging Effects of Marijuana Prohibition

- Because vigorous enforcement of the marijuana laws forces the roughest, toughest criminals to take over marijuana trafficking, **prohibition causes violence** and increases predatory crime.

- Prohibition invites corruption within the criminal justice system by giving officials easy, tempting opportunities to accept bribes, steal and sell marijuana, and plant evidence on innocent people.

- By placing marijuana in an unregulated, underground drug market, prohibition creates additional health hazards from impure or contaminated marijuana.

- By lumping marijuana in with harder drugs, prohibition thwarts realistic drug education and fosters irresponsible drug consumption.

MPP has already Succeeded in Changing Policy

MPP orchestrated testimony before the U.S. Sentencing Commission on March 14, 1995, in support of an amendment to the federal sentencing guidelines to reduce the penalties for marijuana cultivation. On April 10, the commission voted 7-0 in favor of this amendment!

This demonstrates that marijuana policies can be reformed through diligent, focused lobbying.

MPP is also working to mobilize grassroots support through e-mail updates, Internet postings, and communication with MPP members through the monthly *Marijuana Policy Report.*

Prohibition will not be replaced by regulation overnight. MPP is taking the first necessary steps by:

- opposing all harsh, prohibitionist, marijuana-related legislation in the new Congressional crime bills and

- beginning to chip away at the current excesses of marijuana prohibition -- starting with the ban on medicinal marijuana.

The Marijuana Policy Project is working to replace marijuana prohibition with a system that would (1) allow responsible adults to grow their own marijuana and (2) regulate and tax marijuana businesses.

NEW YORK MEDICAL MARIJUANA BILL

On June 11, 2003 the medical marijuana bill, A. 5796, passed the Assembly Codes Committee today by a vote of 13-2. The bill, which would allow seriously ill patients to use medical marijuana with their doctors' recommendations without fear of arrest or jail, was aided by a show of support from New York's medical community. A statement signed by more than 1,100 New York doctors, declaring that "seriously ill people should not be subject to criminal sanctions for using marijuana if the patient's physician has told the patient that such use is likely to be beneficial," was published as a full-page ad in the *Legislative Gazette*.

In addition, the bill has been endorsed by both the New York State Nurses Association and the New York State Association of County Health Officials. NYSACHO's statement reads in part:

> Marijuana has proven to be effective in the treatment of people with HIV/AIDS, multiple sclerosis, cancer, and those suffering from severe pain or nausea. The Institute of Medicine (IOM) report, *Marijuana and Medicine: Assessing the Science Base*, concluded that medical use of marijuana is less dangerous and less addictive than cocaine, morphine and methamphetamines, all of which are legally available.

MEDICAL MARIJUANA FACTS

- Eight states -- Alaska, California, Colorado, Hawaii, Maine, Nevada, Oregon and Washington -- currently have laws protecting medical marijuana patients from arrest and jail.

- Tens of thousands of patients nationwide -- people with AIDS, cancer, glaucoma, and multiple sclerosis -- are *already* using marijuana to treat their symptoms.

- *Presently, patients can be arrested and sent to prison for using marijuana* – even those who have their doctors' approval.
  - The federal penalty for possessing one joint is up to one year in prison, and the penalty for growing one plant is up to five years.[44] And a medical need is no excuse.

- The vast majority of Americans support legal access to medical marijuana.
  - For example, an ABC News/Discovery News poll released on May 29, 1997, found that 69% of American adults support "legalizing medical use of marijuana"; and a Family Research Council survey

---

[44] 21 U.S.C. 844 and 841(b)(1)(D).

released on June 18, 1997, found that 74% of the respondents agreed with the statement, "People who find that marijuana is effective for their medical condition should be able to use it legally."

- A 1990 scientific survey found that 54% of oncologists with an opinion favored the controlled availability of marijuana, and 44% had already broken the law by suggesting at least once that a patient obtain marijuana illegally.[45]

- The FBI reports a total of 695,201 marijuana arrests in 1997 -- the highest total in U.S. history -- 87% of which were for possession.[46] More than 10 million marijuana users have been arrested since 1968. If only 1% of these people were using marijuana medicinally, then there have been 100,000 patients arrested since 1968! (see figure 1)

- Numerous organizations have recently taken positions in support of legal access to medical marijuana and/or opposing the criminalization of medical marijuana-using patients, including:
  - AIDS Action Council, American Academy of Family Physicians, American Bar Association, American Public Health Association, California Medical Association, California Legislative Council for Older Americans, California Pharmacists Association, California Society of Addiction Medicine, *Consumer Reports* magazine, Lymphoma Foundation of America, Multiple Sclerosis California Action Network, National Association of People With AIDS, the *New England Journal of Medicine*, and several state Nurses Associations (e.g., California, New York, and Virginia).[47]

---

[45] Doblin and Kleiman, "Marijuana as Antiemetic Medicine," *Journal of Clinical Oncology, 9,* 1991; Pp. 1314-1319

[46] *Crime in the United States: 1997,* FBI's division of Uniform Crime Reports; Washington, D.C.: U.S. Government Printing Office, 1998; Pp. 221-222.

[47] These and other organizations' positions are available from the Marijuana Policy Project Foundation.

Figure 1: New Marijuana Arrest Record

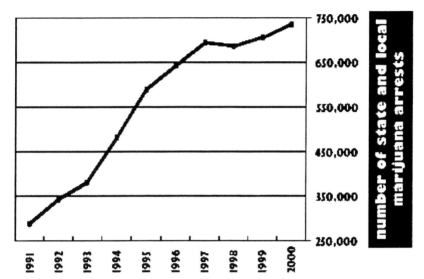

In 2000, the number of marijuana arrests in the United States (by state and local police) was the largest in history: 734,498! And 88% of those arrests were for possession, not sale or manufacture. (Source: FBI's division of Uniform Crime Reports, *Crime in the United States: 2000,* published in October 2001.)

FREQUENTLY ASKED QUESTIONS: MARIJUANA FOR MEDICAL PURPOSES IN CANADA

New Regulatory Approach

Why is Health Canada developing a new regulatory approach now?
On July 31, 2000, the Court of Appeal for Ontario rendered its decision in the case of Terrance Parker who uses marijuana to help control his epilepsy. The Court dealt exclusively with the issue of medical use of marijuana. In a companion case, the same Court concluded that Parliament can validly prohibit marijuana where used for recreational purposes. The Court upheld a 1997 lower court decision to stay the charges against Mr. Parker on constitutional grounds and raised issues related to the section 56 process, such as the broad discretion given by the law to the Minister of Health to grant exemptions, transparency of the process and what constitutes medical necessity. As a result, the Court declared the prohibition on the possession of marijuana in the Controlled Drugs and

Substances Act (CDSA) to be unconstitutional and of no force and effect. The declaration of invalidity was suspended for a year, however, to avoid leaving a gap in the regulatory scheme.

Will the Government of Canada appeal the decision of R. v. Parker?

The decision on whether or not to appeal lies with the Attorney General of Canada. September 29, 2000 is the deadline to file a motion seeking leave to appeal to the Supreme Court of Canada.

It is important not to confuse the issues. The possible need to seek leave to appeal on the narrow legal issues that do not relate directly to the medical use of marijuana does not detract from the Government's commitment to create a framework that will support those who need marijuana for medical purposes. The announcement today relates to the creation of such an approach irrespective of whether an appeal has to be launched or not.

Will concerns from key stakeholders be considered?

When making the regulatory changes, Health Canada has and will continue to take into account concerns raised by key stakeholders such as health care providers, pharmacists, hospitals, provincial licensing authorities, care givers, law enforcement officials and their agencies, addiction agencies, and those using the drug for medical purposes.

When will the new regulatory approach be in place and what is the process for amending or developing regulations?

Health Canada intends to have the new regulatory approach in place by July 31, 2001. Key steps in developing or amending regulations include:

- New draft regulations are prepared based on the policy developed (which takes into account issues and concerns raised by key stakeholders).

- Once approved by the Governor in Council, the draft regulations are published in the Canada Gazette Part I and comments from the public are requested.

- The regulations are amended where appropriate and re-submitted to the Governor in Council for approval and publication in Canada Gazette Part II.

- The new regulations take effect on the date specified in the regulations or on the date of registration.

Is this the first step towards the legalization of marijuana?
No. The regulatory approach centers around the process of providing access to marijuana for medical purposes. Marijuana still remains an illegal drug in Canada.

How does this verdict affect other provinces and territories?
This verdict only applies to Ontario. However, the new regulatory approach developed by Health Canada will apply to individuals in all provinces.

The Current Process for Marijuana for Medical Purposes

How can Canadians access marijuana for medical purposes?
Currently and until the new regulatory approach is in place, individuals who wish to use marijuana for medical purposes can still apply under section 56 of the CDSA to obtain an exemption.

What is section 56 of the Controlled Drugs and Substances Act (CDSA)?
Section 56 of the CDSA gives the Minister of Health the authority to grant exemptions if, in the opinion of the Minister, such an exemption is necessary for a medical or scientific purpose or is otherwise in the public interest. Such an exemption permits certain activities that are otherwise prohibited by the Act or its Regulations (e.g. the cultivation and possession of marijuana).

How does an individual apply for an exemption
to use marijuana for a medical purpose?
An application for an exemption must be submitted in writing to the Minister of Health and specify the activity for which the exemption is sought. A statement from the treating physician in support of the application along with details on the patient's medical and drug therapy histories must also be included with the application. An interim guidance document and application form are available online.

How are applications reviewed?
Because the circumstances of each applicant are unique, applications are reviewed on a case-by-case basis. The review takes into consideration the medical necessity of the applicant.

How does the R. v. Parker verdict affect current exemptees?
Exemptions granted under the CDSA remain valid. The Court suspended its declaration of invalidity with respect to the possession of marijuana. As the

marijuana prohibition remains in full force and effect, exemptees should continue to carry their letters of exemption with them at all times.

Clinical Trials and Canadian Supply

Is marijuana a safe and effective drug?

Marijuana is not approved as a drug in any country in the world. Health Canada is sponsoring a variety of research activities to evaluate the safety and efficacy of smoked marijuana and of cannabinoids. In this regard, a request for proposal (RFP) was jointly developed by Health Canada and the Canadian Institutes of Health Research. This research is expected to span five years.

Where will the marijuana come from for the research?

Health Canada recognizes the need for standardized quality marijuana for research purposes from a Canadian legal supplier. Through Public Works and Government Services Canada (PWGSC), a request for proposal (RFP) was released on May 5, 2000. The RFP looks to establish a Canadian source of quality, standardized, affordable, research-grade marijuana. The requirement for this source was originally outlined in Health Canada's Research Plan for Marijuana for Medical Purposes, released June 9, 1999.

Who will be receiving the marijuana from the legal supplier?

The RFP was designed to produce quality, standardized, affordable, research-grade marijuana to be used for scientific research in Canada. Therefore, the marijuana will be made available to qualified, approved scientists for research.

How soon will the marijuana be made available to the eligible recipients/participants in the research projects?

The first production quantities should be made available for qualified research projects within one year after awarding the contract, as stipulated in the RFP.

Why can't marijuana that is seized by law enforcement be used for research purposes?

As the source and quality of the drug is seldom known, the risks to humans cannot be easily evaluated. There is uncertainty about contaminants such as herbicides and pesticides which could be detrimental to health. In addition, the Commission of Narcotic Drugs General Assembly has adopted a resolution to encourage countries, including Canada, to refrain from supplying confiscated drugs for any purpose.

Chapter 2

MEDICAL UTILITY OF MARIJUANA[*]

William T. Beaver, Julie Buring, Avram Goldstein,
Kenneth Johnson, Reese Jones, Mark G. Kris,
Kathi Mooney, Paul Palmberg and John Phair

INTRODUCTION

On February 19 and 20, 1997, the National Institutes of Health (NIH) held a meeting concerning the potential medical uses of marijuana. Ballot initiatives in California and Arizona had sparked a public health and policy debate on the medical utility of marijuana and the desirability of allowing healthcare providers to prescribe, and patients to receive, marijuana for medicinal purposes.

For some years the principal psychoactive ingredient of marijuana, delta-9-tetrahydrocannabinol (^{9}-THC), has been available to healthcare providers in an oral form as dronabinol (trade name Marinol) for the treatment of emesis associated with cancer chemotherapy and for appetite stimulation in the treatment of AIDS wasting syndrome. The current debate centers primarily on the potential for other treatment indications and the claims that, when smoked, marijuana offers therapeutic advantages over the currently available oral form. As the Federal Government's principal biomedical research agency, the NIH believed that the public debate could benefit from an impartial examination of all the data available

---

[*] Excerpted from the National Institute of Health website: www.nih.gov.

to date concerning these issues. As the claims for benefits were wide ranging, 10 major components of the NIH participated in the planning for the conference.

The NIH planning group focused the meeting on the following four questions concerning marijuana as a potential therapeutic agent:

- *Question 1* - What research has been done previously and what is currently known about the possible medical uses of marijuana?

- *Question 2* - What are the major unanswered scientific questions?

- *Question 3* - What are the diseases or conditions for which marijuana might have potential as a treatment and that merit further study?

- *Question 4* - What special issues have to be considered in conducting clinical studies of the therapeutic uses of marijuana?

The meeting was formatted as a scientific workshop. It was not an attempt to render a consensus. Therefore, it was structured so that speakers with experience in the relevant therapeutic areas would present to a group of eight expert consultants who possessed broad expertise in clinical studies and therapeutics and who had no public positions on the potential use of marijuana as a therapeutic agent. Each presentation was followed by a session for questions and answers from the Expert Group. The second day was allotted for the public to present their views and for discussion by the Expert Group. This report represents a compilation of the views of the Expert Group. Since this report was not intended as a general review of the literature on marijuana and THC, only a few selected references from among the thousands that exist are cited. Each of the members in the Expert Group chose those references relevant to their own contributions to the report.

CLINICAL PHARMACOLOGY OF MARIJUANA

The Pharmacology of Natural Products

It is important to keep in mind that marijuana is not a single drug. Marijuana is a mixture of the dried flowering tops and leaves from the plant cannabis sativa (Agurell et al. 1984; Graham 1976; Jones 1987; Mechoulam 1973). Like most plants, marijuana is a variable and complex mixture of biologically active compounds (Agurell et al. 1986; Graham 1976; Mechoulam 1973). Characterizing the clinical pharmacology of the constituents in any pharmacologically active plant is often complicated, particularly when the plant is smoked or eaten more or less in its natural form. Marijuana is not unusual in this respect. Cannabis sativa is a very adaptive plant, so its characteristics are even more variable than most plants (Graham 1976; Mechoulam 1973). Some of the seeming inconsistency or uncertainty in scientific reports describing the clinical pharmacology of marijuana results from the inherently variable potency of the plant material used in research studies. Inadequate control over drug dose when researching the effects of smoked and oral marijuana, together with the use of research subjects who vary greatly in their past experience with marijuana, contribute differing accounts of what marijuana does or does not do.

The Plant

Marijuana contains more than 400 chemicals. Approximately 60 are called cannabinoids; i.e., C_{21} terpenes found in the plant and their carboxylic acids, analogs, and transformation products (Agurell et al. 1984, 1986; Mechoulam 1973). Most of the naturally occurring cannabinoids have been identified. Cannabinoids appear in no other plant. Cannabinoids have been the subject of much research, particularly since the mid 1960s when Mechoulam and his colleagues first isolated delta-9-tetrahydrocannabinol (^{9}-THC) (Mechoulam 1973; Mechoulam et al. 1991). THC in the scientific literature is termed ^{9}-THC or ^{1}-THC depending on whether the pyran or monoterpinoid numbering system is used.

Cannabinoids of Importance

THC, the main psychoactive cannabinoid in marijuana, is an optically active resinous substance. THC is not soluble in water but is extremely lipid soluble (Agurell et al. 1984, 1986; Mechoulam 1973). Varying proportions of other cannabinoids, mainly cannabidiol (CBD) and cannabinol (CBN), are also present in marijuana, sometimes in quantities that might modify the pharmacology of THC or cause effects of their own. CBD is not psychoactive but has significant anticonvulsant, sedative, and other pharmacologic activity likely to interact with THC (Adams and Martin 1996; Agurell et al. 1984, 1986; Hollister 1986*a).*

The concentration of THC and other cannabinoids in marijuana varies greatly depending on growing conditions, plant genetics, and processing after harvest

(Adams and Martin 1996; Agurell et al. 1984; Graham 1976; Mechoulam 1973). In the usual mixture of leaves and stems distributed as marijuana, concentration of THC ranges from 0.3 percent to 4 percent by weight. However, specially grown and selected marijuana can contain 15 percent or more THC. Thus, a marijuana cigarette weighing 1 gram (g) might contain as little as 3 milligrams (mg) of THC or as much as 150 mg or more.

Potency of Tetrahydrocannabinol

THC is quite potent when compared to most other psychoactive drugs. An intravenous (IV) dose of only a milligram or two can produce profound mental and physiologic effects (Agurell et al. 1984, 1986; Fehr and Kalant 1983; Jones 1987). Large doses of THC delivered by marijuana or administered in the pure form can produce mental and perceptual effects similar to drugs usually termed hallucinogens or psychomimetics. However, the way marijuana is used in the United States does not commonly lead to such profound mental effects. Despite potent psychoactivity and pharmacologic actions on multiple organ systems, cannabinoids have remarkably low lethal toxicity. Lethal doses in humans are not known. Given THC's potency on some brain functions, the clinical pharmacology of marijuana containing high concentrations of THC, for example greater than 10 percent, may well differ from plant material containing only 1 or 2 percent THC simply because of the greater dose delivered.

Some Limitations of Previous Marijuana Research

Unfortunately, much of what is known about the human pharmacology of smoked marijuana comes from experiments with plant material containing about 2 percent THC or less, or occasionally up to 4 percent THC. In addition, human experiments typically are done in laboratory settings where only one or two smoked doses were administered to relatively young, medically screened, healthy male volunteers well experienced with the effects of marijuana. Females rarely participated in past marijuana research because of prohibitions (now removed) against their inclusion. Thus the clinical pharmacology of single or repeated smoked marijuana doses given to older people or to people with serious diseases has hardly been researched at all in a controlled laboratory or clinic setting. Some of the very few reports of experiments that have included older or sicker people, particularly patients less experienced in using marijuana, suggest the profile of adverse effects may differ from healthy student volunteers smoking in a laboratory experiment (Hollister 1986a, 1988a).

THC administered alone in its pure form is the most thoroughly researched cannabinoid. Much of what is written about the clinical pharmacology of marijuana is actually inferred from the results of experiments using only pure THC. Generally, in experiments actually using marijuana, the assumed dose of marijuana was based only on the concentration of THC in the plant material. The amounts of cannabidiol and other cannabinoids in the plant also vary so that pharmacologic interactions modifying the effects THC may occur when marijuana is used instead of pure THC. Only rarely in human experiments using marijuana was the content of CBD or other cannabinoids specified or the possibility of interactive effects between THC and other cannabinoids or other marijuana constituents actually measured.

The result of this research strategy is that a good deal is known about the pharmacology of THC, but experimental confirmation that the pharmacology of a marijuana cigarette is indeed entirely or mainly determined by the amount of THC it contains remains to be completed. The scientific literature contains occasional hints that the pharmacology of pure THC, although similar, is not always the same as the clinical pharmacology of smoked marijuana containing the same amount of THC (Graham 1976; Harvey 1985; Institute of Medicine 1982). Proponents of therapeutic applications of marijuana emphasize possible but not well documented or proven differences between the effects of the crude plant and pure constituents like THC (Grinspoon and Bakalar 1993).

Route-Dependent Pharmacokinetics

Route of administration determines the pharmacokinetics of the cannabinoids in marijuana, particularly absorption and metabolism (Adams and Martin 1996; Agurell et al. 1984, 1986). Typically, marijuana is smoked as a cigarette (a joint) weighing between 0.5 and 1.0 g, or in a pipe in a way not unlike tobacco smoking. Marijuana can also be baked in foods and eaten, or ethanol or other extracts of plant material can be taken by mouth. Some users claim marijuana containing adequate THC can be heated without burning and the resulting vapor inhaled to produce the desired level of intoxication. This has not been studied under controlled conditions. Pure preparations of THC and other cannabinoids can be administered by mouth, by rectal suppository, by IV injection, or smoked. IV injection of crude extracts of marijuana plant material would be quite toxic, however.

Marijuana Smoking and Oral Administration

Smoking plant material is a special way of delivering psychoactive drugs to the brain. Smoking has different behavioral and physiologic consequences than oral or IV administration. What is well known about tobacco (nicotine) and coca (cocaine) clinical psychopharmacology and toxicity illustrates this point all too well. When marijuana is smoked, THC in the form of an aerosol in the inhaled smoke is absorbed within seconds and delivered to the brain rapidly and efficiently as would be expected of a very lipid-soluble drug. Peak venous blood levels of 75 to 150 nanograms per milliliter (ng/mL) of plasma appear about the time smoking is finished (Agurell et al. 1984, 1986; Huestis et al. 1992a, 1992b). Arterial concentrations of THC have not been measured but would be expected to be much higher initially than venous levels, as is the case with smoked nicotine or smoked cocaine.

Oral ingestion of THC or marijuana is quite different than smoking. Maximum THC and other cannabinoid blood levels are only reached 1 to 3 hours after an oral dose (Adams and Martin 1996; Agurell et al. 1984, 1986). Onset of psychoactive and other pharmacologic effects is rapid after smoking but much slower after oral doses.

Marijuana Smoking Behavior and Dose Control

As with any smoked drug (e.g., nicotine or cocaine), characterizing the pharmacokinetics of THC and other cannabinoids from smoked marijuana is a challenge (Agurell et al. 1986; Heishman et al. 1989; Herning et al. 1986; Heustis et al. 1992a). A person's smoking behavior during an experiment is difficult for a researcher to control. People differ. Smoking behavior is not easily quantified. An experienced marijuana smoker can titrate and regulate dose to obtain the desired acute psychological effects and to avoid overdose and/or minimize undesired effects. Each puff delivers a discrete dose of THC to the body. Puff and inhalation volume changes with phase of smoking, tending to be highest at the beginning and lowest at the end of smoking a cigarette. Some studies found frequent users to have higher puff volumes than did less frequent marijuana users. During smoking, as the cigarette length shortens, the concentration of THC in the remaining marijuana increases; thus, each successive puff contains an increasing concentration of THC.

One consequence of this complicated process is that an experienced marijuana smoker can regulate almost on a puff-by-puff basis the dose of THC delivered to lungs and thence to brain. A less experienced smoker is more likely to overdose or underdose. Thus a marijuana researcher attempting to control or specify dose in a pharmacologic experiment with smoked marijuana has only partial control over drug dose actually delivered. Postsmoking assay of cannabinoids in blood or urine can partially quantify dose actually absorbed after smoking, but the analytic procedures are methodologically demanding, and only in recent years have they become at all practical.

After smoking, venous blood levels of THC fall precipitously within minutes, and an hour later they are about 5 to 10 percent of the peak level (Agurell et al. 1986; Huestis et al. 1992a, 1992b). Plasma clearance of THC is quite high, 950 milliliters per minute (mL/min) or greater; thus approximating hepatic blood flow. However, the rapid disappearance of THC from blood is largely due to redistribution to other tissues in the body rather than simply because of rapid cannabinoid metabolism (Agurell et al. 1984, 1986). Metabolism in most tissues is relatively slow or absent. Slow release of THC and other cannabinoids from tissues and subsequent metabolism makes for a very long elimination half-time. The terminal half-life of THC is estimated to be from about 20 hours to as long as 10 to 13 days, though reported estimates vary as expected with any slowly cleared substance and the use of assays with varied sensitivity.

Cannabinoid metabolism is extensive with at least 80 probably biologically inactive but not completely studied metabolites formed from THC alone (Agurell et al. 1986; Hollister 1988a). 11-hydroxy-THC is the primary active THC metabolite. Some inactive carboxy metabolites have terminal half-lives of 50 hours to 6 days or more and thus serve as long persistence markers of prior marijuana use by urine tests. Most of the absorbed THC dose is eliminated in feces and about 33 percent in urine. THC enters enterohepatic circulation and undergoes hydroxylation and oxidation to 11-nor-9-carboxy-delta-9-THC (9-COOH- ^{9}-THC). The glucuronide is excreted as the major urine metabolite along with about 18 nonconjugated metabolites. Frequent and infrequent marijuana users are similar in the way they metabolize THC (Agurell et al. 1986; Kelly and Jones 1992).

Route of Use Bioavailability and Dose

THC bioavailability, i.e., the actual absorbed dose as measured in blood, from smoked marijuana varies greatly among individuals. Bioavailability can range from 1 percent to 24 percent with the fraction absorbed rarely exceeding 10 percent to 20 percent of the THC in a marijuana cigarette or pipe (Agurell et al.

1986; Hollister 1988*a*). This relatively low and quite variable bioavailability results from significant loss of THC in sidestream smoke, from variation in individual smoking behaviors, from incomplete absorption from inhaled smoke, and from metabolism in lung and cannabinoid pyrolysis. A smoker's experience is probably an important determinant of dose actually absorbed (Herning et al. 1986; Johansson et al. 1989). Much more is known about the dynamics of tobacco (nicotine) smoking. Many of the same pharmacokinetic considerations apply to marijuana smoking.

Oral bioavailability of THC, whether given in the pure form or as THC in marijuana, also is low and extremely variable, ranging between 5 percent and 20 percent (Agurell et al. 1984, 1986). Great variation can occur even when the same individual is repeatedly dosed under controlled and ideal conditions. THC's low and variable oral bioavailability is largely a consequence of large first-pass hepatic elimination of THC from blood and due to erratic absorption from stomach and bowel. Because peak effects are slow in onset and variable in intensity, typically at least an hour or two after an oral dose, it is more difficult for a user to titrate dose than with marijuana smoking. When smoked, THC's active metabolite 11-hydroxy-THC probably contributes little to the effects since relatively little is formed, but after oral doses the amounts of 11-hydroxy-THC metabolite may exceed that of THC and thus contribute to the pharmacologic effects of oral THC or marijuana.

Mental and Behavioral Effects

Common Acute Effects
Usually the mental and behavioral effects of marijuana consist of a sense of well-being (often termed euphoria or a high), feelings of relaxation, altered perception of time and distance, intensified sensory experiences, laughter, talkativeness, and increased sociability when taken in a social setting. Impaired memory for recent events, difficulty concentrating, dreamlike states, impaired motor coordination, impaired driving and other psychomotor skills, slowed reaction time, impaired goal-directed mental activity, and altered peripheral vision are common associated effects (Adams and Martin 1996; Fehr and Kalant 1983; Hollister 1988*a*; Institute of Medicine 1982; Tart 1971).

With repeated exposure, varying degrees of tolerance rapidly develops to many subjective and physiologic effects (Fehr and Kalant 1983; Jones 1987). Thus, intensity of acute effects is determined not only by THC dose but also by past experience, setting, expectations, and poorly understood individual differences in sensitivity. After a single moderate smoked dose most mental and behavioral effects are easily measurable for only a few hours and are usually no longer measurable after 4 to 6 hours (Hollister 1986a, 1988a). A few published reports describe lingering cognitive or behavioral changes 24 hours or so after a single smoked or oral dose (Fehr and Kalant 1983; Institute of Medicine 1982; Yesavage et al. 1985). Venous blood levels of THC or other cannabinoids correlate poorly with intensity of effects and character of intoxication (Agurell et al. 1986; Barnett et al. 1985; Huestis et al. 1992a).

Adverse Mental Effects

Large smoked or oral marijuana doses or even ordinary doses taken by a sensitive, inexperienced, or predisposed person can produce transient anxiety, panic, feelings of depression and other dysphoric mood changes, depersonalization, bizarre behaviors, delusions, illusions, or hallucinations (Adams and Martin 1996; Fehr and Kalant 1983; Hollister 1986a, 1988a; Institute of Medicine 1982). Depending on the mix of symptoms and behaviors, the state has been termed an acute panic reaction, toxic delirium, acute paranoid state, or acute mania. The unpleasant effects are usually of sudden onset, during or shortly after smoking, or appear more gradually an hour or two after an oral dose, usually last a few hours, less often a few days, and completely clear without any specific treatment other than reassurance and a supportive environment. A subsequent marijuana dose, particularly a lower one, may be well tolerated. In a large survey of regular marijuana users, 17 percent of young adult respondents reported experiencing at least one of the preceding symptoms during at least one occasion of marijuana use, usually early in their use (Tart 1971).

Whether marijuana can produce or trigger lasting mood disorders (depression or mania) or schizophrenia is less clearly established (Fehr and Kalant 1983; Gruber and Pope 1994; Hollister 1986a, 1988a; Institute of Medicine 1982). A psychotic state with schizophrenic-like and manic features lasting a week or more has been described. Marijuana can clearly worsen schizophrenia. Chronic marijuana use can be associated with behavior characterized by apathy and loss of motivation along with impaired educational performance even without obvious behavioral changes (Pope and Yurgelun-Todd 1996; Pope et al. 1995). The explanation and mechanisms for this association are still not well established.

Cardiovascular and Autonomic Effects

A consistent, prominent, and sudden effect of marijuana is a 20 to 100 percent increase in heart rate lasting up to 2 to 3 hours (Hollister 1986a, 1988a; Jones 1985). After higher smoked or oral doses postural hypotension and associated faintness or dizziness can occur upon standing up from a supine or prone position. Tolerance to these effects appears after only a few days of two to three times per day dosing (Benowitz and Jones 1981; Jones 1985). Typical is a modest increase in supine blood pressure. Cardiac output can increase 30 percent when supine. Peripheral vascular resistance decreases with the greatest drop in resistance in skeletal muscles. Skin temperature drops are large; 4 to 6 degrees centigrade, even after a modest smoked dose and roughly parallel to plasma norepinephrine increases. With a few days of repeated exposure to frequent doses of oral THC or marijuana extract, supine blood pressure falls, the sometimes marked initial orthostatic hypotension disappears, blood volume increases, and heart rate slows (Benowitz and Jones 1981). Thus like other system effects, the intensity and character of many hemodynamic effects of single smoked doses in humans are a function of recent marijuana exposure, dose, and even body position.

The cardiovascular effects of smoked or oral marijuana have not presented any health problems for healthy and relatively young users. However, marijuana smoking by older patients, particularly those with some degree of coronary artery or cerebrovascular disease, is likely to pose greater risks because of the resulting increased cardiac work, increased catecholamines, carboxyhemoglobin, and postural hypotension (Benowitz and Jones 1981; Hollister 1988a). Such issues have not been well addressed in past marijuana research.

Respiratory System Effects

Pulmonary effects associated with marijuana smoking include transient bronchodilation after acute exposure. Chronic bronchitis and pharyngitis are associated with repeated exposure with an increased frequency of pulmonary illness. With chronic marijuana smoking, large-airway obstruction is evident on pulmonary function tests, and cellular inflammatory histopathological abnormalities appear in bronchial epithelium (Adams and Martin 1996; Hollister 1986a). These effects appear to be additive to those produced by tobacco smoking.

Endocrine System

Endocrine system effects include a moderate depression of spermatogenesis and sperm motility and a decrease in plasma testosterone in males. Prolactin, FSH, LH, and GH levels are decreased in females. Although suppressed ovulation and other ovulatory cycle changes occur in nonhuman primates, a study of human females smoking marijuana in a research hospital setting did not find hormone or menstrual cycle changes like those in the monkeys given THC (Mendelson and Mello 1984; Mendelson et al. 1984a). Relatively little research has been done on experimentally administered marijuana effects on human female endocrine and reproductive system function.

Immune System

THC and other cannabinoids in marijuana have immunosuppressant properties producing impaired cell-mediated and humoral immune system responses. A large literature describes the results of experiments with animal and animal tissue in in vivo and in vitro model systems. THC and other cannabinoids suppress antibody formation, cytokine production, leukocyte migration and natural killer-cell activity. Cannabinoids decrease host resistance to infection from bacterial and viral infection in animals. Marijuana smokers show evidence of impaired immune function: for example, decreased leukocyte blastogenesis in response to mitogens. Marijuana smokers, when compared to nonmarijuana smokers, have more respiratory illness (Polen et al. 1993).

The cannabinoids have been characterized as immunomodulators because although they generally suppress, they occasionally enhance some immune responses (Friedman et al. 1995). Reviews of marijuana immune system effects have characterized the effects as complicated or conflicting or controversial (Adams and Martin 1996; Hollister 1988b). The clinical significance or relevance of these findings remains uncertain. Much of the complexity and controversy results from the use of mostly in vitro animal models, or in vitro animal and human cell cultures, or in vivo animal studies. Generally in most studies the cannabinoid doses or concentrations used have been quite high when compared to reasonable levels of exposure in human marijuana smoking.

Suppressed or impaired immune mechanisms would likely have negative effects on health by increasing susceptibility to infection or to tumors. People with compromised immune systems or existing malignancies may be at higher risk than healthy people. For example, the risk of developing AIDS may be higher with HIV infection, with a higher risk for infection by opportunistic bacteria, fungi, or viruses. On the other hand, some have suggested that the immunosuppressive effects of cannabinoids might be useful clinically; for example, in treating multiple sclerosis, mostly reasoning from theoretical assumptions or experimental disease models in animals.

In summary, there is good evidence that THC and other cannabinoids can impair both cell-mediated and humoral immune system functioning, leading to decreased resistance to infection by viruses and bacteria. However, the health relevance of these findings to human marijuana use remains uncertain. Conclusive evidence for increased malignancy, or enhanced acquisition of HIV, or the development of AIDS, has not been associated with marijuana use.

There is a need for further research, particularly in circumstances where long-term administration of marijuana might be considered for therapeutic purposes; for example, in individuals who are HIV-positive or who have tumors, malignancies, or diseases where immune system function may be important in the genesis of the disease. Clinical studies with smoked marijuana in patients with compromised immune systems may offer a sensitive index of adverse immune system effects associated with cannabinoid exposure. Direct measures of viral load and other sensitive indices of immune system function are now more practical than in past years when most of the cannabinoid immune system research was carried out. The possibility that frequent and prolonged marijuana use might lead to clinically significant impairments of immune system function is great enough that such studies should be part of any marijuana medication development research, particularly when marijuana will be used by patients with compromised immune systems.

Tolerance and Physical Dependence

After repeated smoked or oral marijuana doses, marked tolerance is rapidly acquired (after a day or two) to many marijuana effects, e.g., cardiovascular, autonomic, and many subjective effects. After exposure is stopped, tolerance is lost with similar rapidity (Jones et al. 1981). Measurable tolerance or tachyphalaxis is evident for some hours after smoking even a single marijuana cigarette.

Withdrawal symptoms and signs appearing within hours after cessation of repeated marijuana use have been occasionally reported by patients in clinical settings (Duffy and Milin 1996; Mendelson et al. 1984b). A withdrawal syndrome was reliably produced by as little as 5 days of modest but frequent oral doses of THC or marijuana extract in double-blind, placebo-controlled experiments (Jones et al. 1981). THC decreased or relieved the symptoms. Typical symptoms and signs were restlessness, insomnia, irritability, salivation, tearing, nausea, diarrhea, increased body temperature, anorexia, weight loss, tremor, sweating, sleep brainwave rapid eye movement rebound, and subjective sleep disturbance. Increased dreaming contributing to the sleep disturbance sometimes persisted for weeks, but the other signs and symptoms were gone or markedly diminished within 48 hours after the last oral marijuana dose.

Drug Interactions with Marijuana

Tobacco, ethanol, and other psychoactive and therapeutic drugs commonly consumed together with marijuana share metabolic pathways with cannabinoids, so metabolic interactions are likely. Both THC and CBD inhibit the metabolism of drugs metabolized by hepatic mixed-function oxidase enzymes (Benowitz and Jones 1977; Benowitz et al. 1980; Hollister 1986*b*).

The absorption or clearance of other drugs taken with marijuana may be slowed or hastened depending on timing and sequence of drug ingestion and past exposure. For example, ethanol consumed just after smoking a marijuana cigarette produces a much lower peak blood level than the same dose of ethanol taken an hour before marijuana smoking because THC slows gastric emptying time, thus slowing absorption of ethanol.

THC is highly bound to plasma proteins (97 percent to 99 percent) and thus is likely to interact with other highly bound drugs because of competition for binding sites on plasma proteins.

Finally, there is experimental evidence for drug interactions at the functional (neural) adaptation level (Adams and Martin 1996).

By those and possibly by other mechanisms, recent or concurrent THC or CBD exposure measurably alters the pharmacokinetics and/or effects of ethanol, barbiturates, nicotine, amphetamines, cocaine, phencyclidine, opiates, atropine, and clomipramine (Fehr and Kalant 1983; Institute of Medicine 1982). Marijuana use is likely to alter the pharmacology of some concurrently used therapeutic drugs, e.g., cancer chemotherapeutic agents or anticonvulsants.

Cannabinoid Receptors

Mechanisms of psychoactive cannabinoid action were long suspected to be through interactions of/with lipid components of cell membranes (Adams and Martin 1996; Hollister 1988*a*). The discovery of cannabinoid receptors in the human brain in the late 1980s led to renewed interest in the pharmacology and potential therapeutic uses of cannabinoids (Adams and Martin 1996; Herkenham 1992). The mechanisms of action of THC are now assumed to be mainly receptor mediated. So far, it still is a relatively simple receptor family (CB 1 and CB 2). Receptors are abundant in brain areas concerned with memory, cognition, and motor coordination. An endogenous ligand, a fatty acid derivative named anandamide, has been identified but not yet studied in humans (Thomas et al. 1996). A specific THC antagonist, SR141716A, provokes intense withdrawal signs and behaviors in rodents that have been exposed to THC for even relatively brief periods (Adams and Martin 1996). The clinical pharmacology of the antagonist has not been studied in humans.

REFERENCES

Adams, I.B., and Martin, B.R. Cannabis: Pharmacology and toxicology in animals and humans. *Addiction* 91(11):1585-1614, November 1996.

Agurell, S., Dewey, W.L., and Willett, R.E., eds. *The Cannabinoids: Chemical, Pharmacologic, and Therapeutic Aspects.* New York: Academic Press, 1984.

Agurell, S.; Halldin, M.; Lindgren, J.E.; Ohlsson, A.; Widman, M.; Gillespie, H.; and Hollister, L. Pharmacokinetics and metabolism of delta 1-tetrahydrocannabinol and other cannabinoids with emphasis on man. *Pharmacol Rev* 38(1):21-43, March 1986.

Barnett, G.; Licko, V.; and Thompson, T. Behavioral pharmacokinetics of marijuana. *Psychopharmacology* 85(1):51-56, 1985.

Benowitz, N.L., and Jones, R.T. Effect of delta-9-tetrahydrocannabinol on drug distribution and metabolism: Antipyrine, pentobarbital and ethanol. *Clin Pharmacol Ther* 22(3):259-268, 1977.

Benowitz, N.L., and Jones, R.T. Cardiovascular and metabolic considerations in prolonged cannabinoid administration in man. *J Clin Pharmacol* 21:214S-223S, 1981.

Benowitz, N.L.; Nguyen, T.; Jones, R.T.; Herning, R.I.; and Bachman, J. Metabolic and psychophysiologic studies of cannabidiol-hexobarbital interaction. *Clin Pharmacol Ther* 28:115-120, 1980.

Duffy, A., and Milin, R. Case study: Withdrawal syndrome in adolescent chronic cannabis users. *J Am Acad Child Adolesc Psychiatry* 35(12):1618-1621, December 1996.

Fehr, K., and Kalant, H., eds. *ARF/WHO Scientific Meeting on Adverse Health and Behavioral Consequences of Cannabis Use (1981: Toronto, Canada) Cannabis and Health Hazards: Proceedings of an ARF/WHO Scientific Meeting on Adverse Health and Behavioral Consequences of Cannabis Use.* Toronto, Canada: Addiction Research Foundation, 1983.

Friedman, H.; Klein, T.W.; Newton, C.; and Daaka, Y. Marijuana, receptors and immunomodulation. *Adv Exp Med Biol* 373:103-113, 1995.

Graham, J.D.P., ed. *Cannabis and Health.* New York: Academic Press, 1976.

Grinspoon, L., and Bakalar, J.B. *Marihuana, the Forbidden Medicine.* New Haven: Yale University Press, 1993.

Gruber, A.J., and Pope, H.G. Cannabis psychotic disorder: Does it exist? *Am J Addict* v3 (n1):72-83, Winter 1994.

Harvey, D.J., ed. *Satellite Symposium on Cannabis (3rd: 1984: Oxford, England) Marihuana '84: Proceedings of the Oxford Symposium on Cannabis.* Washington, DC: IRL Press, 1985.

Heishman, S.J.; Stitzer, M.L.; and Yingling, J.E. Effects of tetrahydrocannabinol content on marijuana smoking behavior, subjective reports, and performance. *Pharmacol Biochem Behav* 34(1):173-179, September 1989.

Herkenham, M. Cannabinoid receptor localization in brain: Relationship to motor and reward systems. In: Kalivas, P.W., and Samson, H.H., eds. The neurobiology of drug and alcohol addiction. *Ann N Y Acad Sci* 654:19-32, 1992.

Herning, R.I.; Hooker, W.D.; and Jones, R.T. Tetrahydrocannabinol content and differences in marijuana smoking behavior. *Psychopharmacology* 90(2):160-162, 1986.

Hollister, L.E. Health aspects of cannabis. *Pharmacol Rev* 38(1):1-20, March 1986*a*.

Hollister, L.E. Interactions of cannabis with other drugs in man. In: Braude, M.C., and Ginzburg, H.M., eds. *Strategies for Research on the Interactions of Drugs of Abuse.* National Institute on Drug Abuse Research Monograph 68. DHHS Pub. No. (ADM)86-1453. Washington, DC: Supt. of Docs., U.S. Govt. Print. Off., 1986*b*. pp. 110-116.

Hollister, L.E. Cannabis—1988. (Literature review). *Acta Psychiatr Scand* (Suppl) 78(345):108-118, 1988*a*.

Hollister, L.E. Marijuana and immunity. *J Psychoactive Drugs* 20(1:):3-8, January-March 1988*b*.

Huestis, M.A.; Henningfield, J.E.; and Cone, E.J. Blood Cannabinoids. 1. Absorption of THC and formation of 11-OH-THC and THC COOH during and after smoking marijuana. *J Anal Toxicol* 16(5):276-282, September-October 1992*a*.

Huestis, M.A.; Sampson, A.H.; Holicky, B.J.; Henningfield, J.E.; et al. Characterization of the absorption phase of marijuana smoking. *Clin Pharmacol Ther* 52 (1):31-41, July 1992*b*.

Institute of Medicine. *Division of Health Sciences Policy. Marijuana and Health: Report of a Study by a Committee of the Institute of Medicine, Division of Health Sciences Policy.* Washington, DC: National Academy Press, 1982.

Johansson, E.; Halldin, M.M.; Agurell, S.; Hollister, L.E.; and Gillespie, H.K. Terminal elimination plasma half-life of delta 1-tetrahydrocannabinol (delta

1-THC) in heavy users of marijuana. *Eur J Clin Pharmacol* 37(3):273-277, 1989.

Jones, R.T. Drug of abuse profile: Cannabis. *Clin Chem* 33 (11 Suppl):72B-81B, October 1987.

Jones, R.T. Cardiovascular effects of cannabinoids. In: Harvey, D.J., ed. *Marihuana, '84: Proceedings of the Oxford Symposium on Cannabis.* Oxford: IRL Press, 1985. pp. 325-334.

Jones, R.T.; Benowitz, N.L.; and Herning, R.I. Clinical relevance of cannabis tolerance and dependence. *J Clin Pharmacol* 21:143S-152S, 1981.

Kelly, P., and Jones, R.T. Metabolism of tetrahydrocannabinol in frequent and infrequent marijuana users. *J Anal Toxicol* 16:228-235, 1992.

Mechoulam, R., ed. *Marijuana: Chemistry, Pharmacology, Metabolism and Clinical Effects.* New York: Academic Press, 1973.

Mechoulam, R.; Devane, W.A.; Breuer, A.; and Zahalka, J. A random walk through a cannabis field. Special Issue: Pharmacological, chemical, biochemical and behavioral research on cannabis and the cannabinoids. *Pharmacol Biochem Behav* 40(3):461-464, November 1991.

Mendelson, J.H., and Mello, N.K. Effects of marijuana on neuroendocrine hormones in human males and females. In: Braude, M.C., and Ludford, J.P., eds. *Marijuana Effects on the Endocrine and Reproductive Systems.* National Institute on Drug Abuse Research Monograph 44. DHHS Pub. No. (ADM)84-1278. Washington, DC: Supt. of Docs., U.S. Govt. Print. Off., 1984. pp. 97-114.

Mendelson, J.H.; Mello, N.K.; Cristofaro, P.; Ellingboe, J.; and Benedikt, R. Acute effects of marijuana on pituitary and gonadal hormones during the periovulatory phase of the menstrual cycle. In: Harris, L.S., ed. *Problems of Drug Dependence, 1984: Proceedings of the 46th Annual Scientific Meeting, The Committee on Problems of Drug Dependence, Inc. National Institute on Drug Abuse Research Monograph 55.* DHHS Pub. No. (ADM)85-1393. Washington, DC: Supt. of Docs., U.S. Govt. Print. Off., 1984*a*. pp. 24-31.

Mendelson, J.H.; Mello, N.K.; Lex, B.W.; and Bavli, S. Marijuana withdrawal syndrome in a woman. *Am J Psychiatry* 141(10):1289-1290, October 1984*b*.

Polen, M.R.; Sidney, S.; Tekawa, I.S.; Sadler, M.; and Friedman, G.D. Health care use by frequent marijuana smokers who do not smoke tobacco. *West J Med* 158(6):596-601, June 1993.

Pope, H.G., Jr., and Yurgelun-Todd, D. The residual cognitive effects of heavy marijuana use in college students. *JAMA* 275(7):521-527, February 21, 1996.

Pope, H.G.; Gruber, A.J.; and Yurgelun-Todd, D. The residual neuropsychological effects of cannabis: The current status of research. *Drug Alcohol Depend* 38(1):25-34, April 1995.

Tart, C.T. *On Being Stoned: A Psychological Study of Marijuana Intoxication.* Palo Alto, CA: Science and Behavior Books, 1971.

Thomas, B.F.; Adams, I.B.; Mascarella, S.W.; Martin, B.R.; and Razdan, R.K. Structure-activity analysis of anandamide analogs: Relationship to a cannabinoid pharmacophore. *J Med Chem* 39(2):471-497, January 19, 1996.

Yesavage, J.A.; Leirer, V.O.; Denari, M.; and Hollister, L.E. Carry-over effects of marijuana intoxication on aircraft pilot performance: A preliminary report. *Am J Psychiatry* 142(11):1325-1329, November 1985.

Chapter 3

MEDICAL USE OF MARIJUANA: POLICY AND REGULATORY ISSUES

Blanchard Randall IV

HISTORICAL BACKGROUND

Marijuana, or by its botanical name *Cannabis sativa*, has been cultivated worldwide for centuries. The *Cannabis* plant, also raised for the production of hemp fiber, is more generally grown and consumed (smoked) for its medicinal and psychoactive effects. In the United States, historical accounts of the drug's use, both for recreational and medicinal purposes, date back to the nineteenth century and earlier. In those earlier years, marijuana use was legal under state and federal law, but it was smoked more to achieve intoxication than to relieve medical symptoms. By the 1840s, however, marijuana's therapeutic potential gained a modicum of recognition among some U.S. physicians, and from 1850 to the early 1940s the drug was included in the *United States Pharmacopoeia* as a recognized medicinal.[1] Societal opinion about marijuana began to shift in the early 1900s as more and more of the general public and politicians came to believe that use of the drug was connected to the rising crime rate.

---

[1] Bliz, Gregg A. The Medical Use of Marijuana: the Politics of Medicine. *Hamline Journal of Public Law and Policy*, v. 13, spring 1992. p. 118.

By 1935, most states had laws prohibiting either the use, sale, or possession of marijuana. Shortly thereafter, Congress enacted the 1937 Marijuana Tax Act[2] which, rather than outlawing the substance, imposed a tax on its growers, sellers, and buyers. The Act's passage resulted in all medicinal products containing marijuana being withdrawn from the market, and in 1941, the drug was dropped from recognition by *The National Formulary* and *The US. Pharmacopeia.*[3] Possession and sale of the drug remained illegal under state law.

Congressional enactment of the Comprehensive Drug Abuse Prevention and Control Act[4] of 1970 led to an overhaul of existing state and federal statutes governing marijuana. Commonly referred to as the Controlled Substances Act (CSA), it replaced and updated most previous laws concerned with illicit drugs and consolidated them under the jurisdiction of federal control. Existing state laws regulating illicit drugs, though they remained in effect, were overridden by the new federal statute. The CSA established a new system for scheduling all drugs based on their potential for abuse. Under the law, drugs with the highest potential for abuse and no generally accepted medical use, even under the supervision of a licensed physician, were defined as Schedule I drugs. Accordingly, Congress placed marijuana in Schedule I of the Act where it remains to this day.

Despite law enforcement's efforts to control its distribution and use, marijuana has over the years acquired a reputation as the most widely used illicit substance in the nation. At the same time there has evolved a growing body of evidence scientifically documenting the health risks associated with its use. Chronic marijuana smoking can adversely affect the lungs, the cardiovascular system, and possibly the immune and reproductive systems as well. It is also well established that marijuana intoxication can adversely affect a person's coordination, and impair their motor and decision-making skills. Certain psychological health problems and various forms of nefarious behavior have also been associated with use of the drug. In addition, there is the belief, still adhered to by some, that marijuana serves as a "gateway"[5] substance leading to the use of more dangerous drugs, such as cocaine and heroin.

---

[2] In *Leary v. United States*, 395 U.S. 6(1968), the U.S. Supreme Court later declared that portions of the Act were unconstitutional because by requiring citizens to pay a federal tax, particularly for a drug that was illegal under state law, the statute compelled self-incrimination, a violation of the Fifth Amendment.

[3] Ray, Oakley, and Charles Ksir. *Drugs, Society, and Human Behavior.* 8th ed. WCB/McGraw-Hill, 1999. p. 415. (Hereafter cited as Ray, Drugs, Society, and Human Behavior.)

[4] 21 U.S.C., Section 801, et seq.

[5] With respect to the rationale behind the argument that marijuana serves as a "gateway" drug, the Institute of Medicine, in its 1999 report *Marijuana and Medicine: Assessing the Science Base* [cited herein], offered the following: "In the sense that marijuana use typically precedes rather than follows initiation of other illicit drug use, it is indeed a 'gateway' drug. But because

Despite these health ramifications, by the early 1970s, debate over the health consequences of marijuana turned as a growing number of people began smoking the drug as a means of coping with medical problems that were not responsive to conventional medications. In particular, marijuana was being smoked for its alleged therapeutic benefits by patients suffering from acute pain from various causes, cancer, human immunodeficiency virus (HIV), and a host of other medical complications. To supporters of this trend, this is all the clinical and empirical evidence needed to support their view that, for some patients, smoking the drug should be permitted for medical purposes. Moreover, people who have long criticized what they consider to be overly punitive federal anti-drug laws, now argue that these same statutes are sometimes used to make felons out of law-abiding citizens who occasionally smoke marijuana for therapeutic relief.

Opponents of allowing marijuana to be used for medicinal purposes view the debate from an entirely different perspective. They claim that marijuana - whether it is smoked for medicinal or recreational purposes - presents serious behavioral and physiological risks that are neither trivial nor acceptable from a health standpoint. Moreover, they argue that smoked marijuana has not been shown to be safe and effective for treating any medical condition, primarily because its alleged therapeutic utility has yet to be sufficiently demonstrated in well-controlled clinical trials. They challenge the notion that marijuana offers patients medicinal benefits superior to those from conventional pharmaceuticals, and maintain that the drug should not be encouraged for general medical use.

Somewhere between these divergent views lies the opinion of some physicians and scientists that marijuana should at least undergo further scientific evaluation to determine whether it has a legitimate place in medical treatment. To date, only a handful of elected officials have been willing to supported this scientific approach.

Much of the controversy surrounding the medical marijuana issue stems in part from a long-standing disagreement between supporters and government health and law enforcement officials over whether smoking marijuana provides patients a safer and more effective form of treatment than taking oral-dose dronabinol, its synthetic pharmaceutical equivalent. In this report, marijuana refers to the leaves and flowering tops of the Cannabis plant, thought to contain more than 400 different chemicals.[6] At least 60 of these, referred to as cannabinoids, are unique to the cannabis plant. One such cannabinoid, delta-9-

---

underage smoking and alcohol use typically precede marijuana use, marijuana is not the most common, and is rarely the first, 'gateway' to illicit drug use. There is no conclusive evidence that the drug effects of marijuana are causally linked to the subsequent abuse of other illicit drugs."

[6] Ray, Drugs, Society, and Human Behavior, p. 410.

tetrahydrocannabinol or THC, is believed to be the primary chemical component responsible for the drug's psychopharmacological effects. Dronabinol refers to delta-9-tetrahydrocannabinol's synthetic pharmaceutical equivalent.

Dronabinol was first synthesized in the mid-1960s. However, there was little commercial interest in marketing it as a pharmaceutical product until 1981 when its production patents were purchased by the Unimed company.[7] Following clinical trials to affirm its safety and effectiveness, oral-dose dronabinol was approved by the Food and Drug Administration (FDA) in 1985 under its brand-name Marinol for treating nausea experienced by cancer patients undergoing chemotherapy.[8] For enforcement purposes, dronabinol - a controlled substance with some abuse potential of it own -was transferred administratively from Scheduled I to Schedule II of the CSA.[9] The regulatory implications of this change are discussed in the next section of this report.

FEDERAL REGULATION OF MARIJUANA

Drug Enforcement Administration: The Controlled Substances Act

The Controlled Substances Act (CSA), Title II of the Comprehensive Drug Abuse Prevention and Control Act of 1970, is the statute on which the federal government bases most of its authority to regulate what it considers to be harmful and abusable chemical (i.e., drug) substances. The Act is enforced by the Drug Enforcement Administration (DEA), a branch of the Department of Justice. Under the CSA, drugs, referred to statutorily as "controlled substances," are placed into one of five schedules. A substance's scheduling is determined by its potential for abuse, safety concerns, and whether it has a accepted use in medicine.

Drugs, or their chemical precursors, placed in Schedule I are the most restrictively controlled substances covered by the Act. Included in this schedule are such drugs as heroin, other opiate derivatives, hallucinogenic substances (LSD, marijuana, psilocybin, mescaline), and more recently, a host of so-called "designer" drugs such as methylenedioxymethamphetamine, better known as

---

[7] Chakravarty, Subrata N. Pot of Gold. Forbes, September 12, 1983. p. 44. (Hereafter cited as Chakravarty, Pot of Gold)

[8] Russell, Christine. Marijuana-based Drug for Nausea Approved. The Washington Post, Friday, June 7,1985. p. A16.

[9] U.S. Dept. of Justice. Drug Enforcement Administration. Schedules of Controlled Substances: Rescheduling of Synthetic Dronabinol in Sesame Oil and Encapsulated in Soft Gelatin Capsules from Schedule Ito Schedule II; Statement of Policy. Federal Register, v. 51, no. 92, May 13, 1986. p. 17476.

MDMA or Ecstacy. Although Schedule I drugs can be used for experimental and analytical purposes, their unauthorized manufacture, distribution, and/or possession is strictly illegal. To be relegated to Schedule I, a drug or chemical must: have a high potential for abuse; have no currently accepted medical use in treatment in the United States; and lack accepted safety even for [human] use under medical supervision.

Drugs with less potential for abuse, and a recognized medical use, are assigned to Schedules II through V. Most of these are pharmaceutical products, available by prescription only. Drugs [or their primary psychoactive ingredient] placed in Schedule LI are distinguished further by unique restrictions such as annual production quotas and more restrictive limitations on their prescribing. Congress or the Justice Department, through their respective law and rule making authority, can add to, transfer, or remove potentially abusable and dangerous drugs from the five schedules. Under the CSA, before a drug or other substance is assigned to a particular schedule, its potential for abuse, dependence liability, and overall risk to public health, must be determined by the Attorney General. In making this determination, the Attorney General must obtain from the Secretary of Health and Human Services (HHS) a recommendation as to whether the drug should be added [or rescheduled] as a controlled substance. The factors that distinguish the abuse potential characteristics of one schedule from another are shown in the box below, along with examples of drugs typical to each.

When Congress passed the GSA, it placed marijuana along with other well known illegal drugs (e.g., heroin, LSD, etc.) into Schedule I, where most of them remain today. By taking this action, Congress stated de facto that drugs relegated to this schedule were not only highly abusable, but moreover, had no recognized medical use, even for patients being treated by a licensed physician.

Changing current law to allow patients to use marijuana for medicinal purposes raises a host of contentious scientific, regulatory, and political issues. For the drug to be available for general medical use, each of its alleged therapeutic uses would have to be scientifically documented through well designed clinical investigations. In addition to being proven safe and effective, marijuana would have to be rescheduled from Schedule I to Schedule II of the GSA. To justify such a major change in scheduling, both the Justice Department and the Department of Health and Human Services (DHHS) would have to be persuaded that marijuana smoking poses less risk than previously thought, and that the drug has achieved wider therapeutic recognition by the medical profession. Until these policy and regulatory changes coincide, there is little to suggest that the government will modify its longstanding opposition to the drug's use - medical or otherwise.

Schedule I - (A) The drug or other substance has a high potential for abuse; (B) The drug or other substance has no currently accepted medical use in treatment in the United States; (C)There is a lack of accepted safety for use of the drug or other substance under medical supervision. [Examples: heroin, LSD, marijuana, mescaline, methaqualone, phencyclidine, and 3, 4-methylenedioxymethamphetamine, better known as MDMA or Ecstasy.]

Schedule II - (A) The drug or other substance has a high potential for abuse; (B) The drug or other substance has a currently accepted medical use in treatment in the United States or a currently accepted medical use with severe restrictions; (C) Abuse of the drug or other substance may lead to severe psychological or physical dependence. [Examples: codeine, dronabinol (synthetic tetrahydrocannabinol), methadone, opium extracts (morphine), certain sedative/hypnotics, stimulants (cocaine, methamphetamine, methylphenidate).]

Schedule III - (A) The drug or other substance has a potential for abuse less than the drugs or other substances in Schedules I and II; (B) The drug or other substance has a currently accepted medical use in treatment in the United States; (C) Abuse of the drug or other substance may lead to moderate or low physical dependence or high psychological dependence. [Examples: anabolic steroids, certain appetite suppressants, pain medications (aspirin or acetaminophen with codeine), and some barbiturates.]

Schedule IV - (A) The drug or other substance has a low potential for abuse relative to the drugs or other substances in Schedule III; (B) The drug or other substance has a currently accepted medical use in treatment in the United States; (C) Abuse of the drug or other substance may lead to limited physical dependence or psychological dependence relative to the drugs or other substances in Schedule III. [Examples: appetite suppressants, Darvon, anti-anxiety agents (Xanax and Valium).]

Schedule V - (A) The drug or other substance has a low potential for abuse relative to drugs or other substances in Schedule IV; (B) The drug or other substance has a currently accepted medical use in treatment in the United States; (C) Abuse of the drug or other substance may lead to limited physical dependence or psychological dependence relative to the drugs or other substances in Schedule IV. [Examples: cough or cold medications containing lower doses of codeine.]

Source: 21 U.S.C., Section 801. Drug examples are from various sources including: 21 CFR 1308.11 and the Physicians' Desk Reference, 55th ed., 2001.

Food and Drug Administration:
Federal Food, Drug, and Cosmetic Act

The Food and Drug Administration (FDA), an agency of the Public Health Service (PHS) within the DHHS, is responsible for enforcing the nation's food and drug laws governed by the Federal Food, Drug, and Cosmetic Act (FD&C Act). Under this authority, FDA requires that all pharmaceutical products undergo clinical evaluation to determine their safety and effectiveness before they are approved for general medical use. Comprehensive testing is required, regardless of whether the drug is chemically produced in the laboratory or originates from a natural plant or animal source.

Section 201(g)(1) of the FD&C Act defines the term "drug" to mean articles intended for use in the diagnosis, cure, mitigation, treatment, or prevention of disease m man. Under Section 201(p) the term "new drug" is defined as "any drug the composition of which is such that such drug is not generally recognized, among experts qualified by scientific training and experience to evaluate the safety and effectiveness of drugs, as safe and effective for use under the conditions prescribed, recommended, or suggested in the labeling thereof As such, when smoked or otherwise consumed for *therapeutic* purposes, marijuana would also be considered a "new drug in the sense that, under the law, it has yet to become "recognized" as safe and effective by "experts qualified by scientific training and experience." Once a drug has been subjected to sufficient clinical evaluation, and physicians gain more practical experience with its use, its previous status as a new drug can change.

To gain FDA approval, a new drug's safety and effectiveness must be confirmed by "substantial evidence" which is defined as evidence:

> . . . consisting of adequate and well-controlled investigations, including clinical investigations, by experts qualified by scientific training and experience to evaluate the effectiveness of the drug involved, on the basis of which it could fairly and reasonably be concluded by such experts that the drug will have the effect it purports or is represented to have under the conditions of use prescribed, recommended, or suggested in the labeling or proposed labeling thereof.[10]

Conducting such clinical investigations generally requires designing testing protocols that are randomized, blinded, and usually placebo-controlled. Such studies minimize testing bias and greatly enhance the likelihood that the data will be statistically significant, and not the result of random chance. Confirming a

---

[10] 21 U.S.C. 505.

drug's safety and effectiveness is a major undertaking, involving multiple corroborative studies, usually requiring significant financial resources.

Unlike pre-approval studies of drugs intended for oral use, clinical trials using a substance like natural marijuana - which has to be smoked, often have added complications. To conduct such studies, investigators must have a supply of the drug that is virtually "pharmaceutical" like in quality; capable of delivering its primary psychoactive ingredient tetrahydrocannabinol in calibrated milligram doses. Also, since marijuana smoke has an easily discernible taste and smell, researchers and study subjects may find comparing the drug's effects to that of a placebo somewhat problematic. Further, conducting experimental work with controlled substances like marijuana requires compliance with DEA regulatory procedures. By law, Schedule I controlled substances may be used for experimental purposes, but investigators must register with the agency, and abide by its stringent record-keeping and security requirements.

Citizen's Petitions Seeking Marijuana's Rescheduling Under the Controlled Substances Act

Since the early 1970s, advocacy groups have employed a variety of strategies to challenge marijuana's scheduling under the CSA. What started initially as a routine citizen's petition challenging the drug's original scheduling, has evolved into a medico/legal debate that has gone on for the better part of three decades. Although the original citizen's petition was rejected by DEA's predecessor, the Bureau of Narcotics and Dangerous Drugs,[11] the petitioners instigated a succession of appeals, hearing requests, and a variety of other court proceedings.

By the early 1980s, much of the debate and legal maneuvering between government officials and medical marijuana supporters centered on the issue of whether there was sufficient scientific evidence to support the many therapeutic claims being made for smoked marijuana, and whether that evidence met the statutory requirements for a scheduling change. During years of administrative proceedings, advocates have submitted published scientific studies and other data to show that marijuana had pharmacotherapeutic benefits capable of treating a variety of medical conditions. For the most part, the validity of these studies has been challenged by DEA on the grounds that they violated one or more traditional

---

[11] U.S. Dept. of Justice. Bureau of Narcotics and Dangerous Drugs. Schedule of Controlled Substances: Petition to Remove Marijuana or in the Alternative to Control Marijuana in Schedule V of the Controlled Substances Act. *Federal Register*, v. 37, no. 174, September 7,1972. p. 18097.

scientific experimental methods - either that too few patients were involved, the studies were not doubleblind (i.e., research subjects were aware that they were receiving the drug), or they were not conducted in a randomized fashion.

Pro-medical marijuana supporters were largely unsuccessful in their efforts to persuade the Justice Department that the drug has a currently accepted medical use in treatment - or at least a medical use with severe restrictions, until 1988 when a DEA administrative law judge ruled favorably on a petition pending at the time and declared that marijuana's medical use was clear beyond any question. Moreover, he recommended that the drug be made legally available for some medical purposes.[12]

After reconsideration of the judge's recommendation, DEA published a denial of the marijuana rescheduling petition,[13] and announced that it would not accept the opinion that marijuana has an accepted medical use in treatment of some medical conditions. Instead, the agency declared that marijuana must remain in Schedule I of the GSA because it has no accepted medical use in treatment of any condition in the United States, and because it cannot be safely used - even under a doctor's supervision.

The petition denial was appealed and in 1991 the United States Court of Appeals for the District of Columbia Circuit ordered the DEA to reconsider its 1989 decision that marijuana has no currently accepted use in medical treatment in the United States.[14] The judicial panel said the agency acted unreasonably in evaluating the drug's effectiveness for cancer and other seriously ill patients. Nevertheless, after additional review of the entire record, the DEA Administrator issued a final order on March 18, 1992 denying the rescheduling petition once more and reiterating the agency's opinion that natural marijuana has no currently accepted medical use.[15]

The legal confrontation between DEA and proponents of changing U.S. marijuana laws has continued through the 1990s. After DEA issued its final order, the Drug Policy Foundation, the National Organization for the Reform of Marijuana Laws (NORML), and the Alliance for Cannabis Therapeutics (ACT) petitioned the U.S. District Court of Appeals for the District of Columbia seeking a review of DEA's final order declining to reschedule marijuana from Schedule Ito Schedule II of the GSA. In 1994, the D.C. Circuit Court of Appeals held that it

---

[12] Isikoff, Michael. Administrative Judge Urges Medicinal Use of Marijuana. *The Washington Post*, September 7, 1988. p. A2.

[13] U.S. Dept. of Justice. Drug Enforcement Administration. Marijuana Scheduling Petition; Denial of Petition. *Federal Register*, v. 54, no. 249, December 29, 1989. p. 53767.

[14] *Alliance for Cannabis Therapeutics v. DEA*, 930 F. 2d 936 (D.C. Cir. 1991).

[15] U.S. Dept. of Justice. Drug Enforcement Administration. Marijuana Scheduling Petition; Denial of Petition; Remand. *Federal Register*, v. 57, no. 59, March 26, 1992. p. 10499.

would not reconsider ACT's petition for review of DEA's final order.[16] The court cited its previous disposition of the matter in *ACT v. DEA*, 930 F. 2d 936 (D.C. Cir. 1991), upheld the agency's action, and held that on remand, the Administrator had provided a satisfactory explanation of the initial final order.

In 1995, Jon Gettman, a former National Director of NORML, submitted a personal petition to DEA calling for the rescheduling of marijuana. The petition requested that marijuana and all cannabinoids be removed from Schedules I and II of the Controlled Substances Act, based on the claim that the drug does not have the potential for abuse the statute requires for inclusion in those schedules.[17] When a petition calls for the rescheduling of a controlled substance, by law it is referred to the Department of Health and Human Services (HHS) for further scientific and medical evaluation. Based on the HHS evaluation of other relevant data, DEA concluded that there was no substantial evidence that marijuana should be removed from Schedule I. In a letter dated March 20, 2001, DEA Administrator Donnie R. Marshall denied Gettman's petition to initiate rulemaking proceedings to reschedule marijuana.[18]

PREVIOUS GOVERNMENT ACTIONS RELATING TO MARIJUANA

NCI's Past THC Distribution Program

In 1980, the National Cancer Institute (NCI) received approval from FDA and DEA to begin distributing oral doses of THC as an investigational anti-nausea drug for patients receiving chemotherapy.[19] The THC capsules were made available under the Institute's group C guidelines, which were developed originally to allow cancer patients access to promising anticancer drugs - with potential therapeutic value - before they gained official FDA approval for medical use.

The novel program served to make oral THC available nationally to treat nausea in patients undergoing cancer chemotherapy. While the program was

---

[16] Alliance for Cannabis Therapeutics v. DEA, 15 F. 3d 1131 (D.C. Cir. 1994).

[17] National Drug Strategy Network. Petition to Repeal Marijuana Prohibition Filed by Jon Gettman. November 6,1998. [http://www.ndsn.org/NOV95/PETITLON.html]

[18] U.S. Dept. of Justice. Drug Enforcement Administration. Denial of Petition; Notice. *Federal Register*, v. 66, no. 75, April 18, 2001. p. 20037.

[19] Okie, Susan. Cancer Victims to Get Marijuana Ingredient. *The Washington Post*, November11, 1980. p.A1.

operational, encapsulated synthetic THC was distributed through qualified hospitals and clinics. The drug was never made available at retail pharmacies. At the time, the federal government was hoping a pharmaceutical company would come forward and show interest in marketing THC. Reportedly, NCI planned to continue the THC distribution until a drug manufacturer received final FDA approval to sell the drug (see section on FDA's approval of Marinol).[20]

NCI's distribution program was set up to make THC available for treatment purposes, and was not designed to test the drug's safety and efficacy in a controlled clinical trial. In one instance, however, an effort was made to evaluate the overall success of the program in Wisconsin by its Controlled Substances Board.[21] The Board concluded that the state's distribution mechanism was adequate, and confirmed that oral THC was effective in relieving nausea and vomiting. It also noted, however, that adverse central nervous system side effects were prevalent, especially in older patients.

FDA Approves Synthetic Marijuana: Marinol

In 1985, the pharmaceutical firm Unimed received FDA approval to market dronabinol, a synthetically derived form of delta-9-tetrahydrocannabinol (THC), the main psychoactive ingredient in marijuana. Sold under the trade name Marinol, this orally consumed drug was originally approved for the treatment of nausea and vomiting associated with cancer chemotherapy in patients who have failed to respond adequately to conventional antiemetic treatments. As such, Unimed showed substantial evidence that this oral form of THC was safe and effective for its intended use. To accommodate scheduling for the new synthetic form of marijuana, DEA issued a ruling and policy statement transferring dronabinol from Schedule I into Schedule II of the Controlled Substances Act.[22] This regulatory action did not affect the status of natural marijuana or other tetrahydrocannabinols - which remain in Schedule I. Available only by prescription, Marinol's official labeling explains the criteria for determining which chemotherapy patients will be the best candidates for its use, the adverse effects

---

[20] Chakravarty, *Pot of Gold*, p. 44.

[21] Treffert, Darold A., and David E. Joranson. Delta-9-Tetrahydrocannabinol and Therapeutic Research Legislation for Cancer Patients. *Journal of the American Medical Association*, March 18, 1983. p. 1469-1472.

[22] U.S. Dept. of Justice. Drug Enforcement Administration. Schedules of Controlled Substances: Rescheduling of Synthetic Dronobinol in Sesame Oil and Encapsulation in Soft Gelatin Capsules From Schedule Ito Schedule II; Statement of Policy. *Federal Register*, v. 51, no. 92, May 13, 1986. p. 17476.

they may experience, and a warning that use of the drug should be limited to the amount necessary for a single cycle of chemotherapy of a few days duration.

Subsequent clinical investigations confirmed an earlier hypothesis that synthetic marijuana might also be a valuable appetite stimulant for treating acquired immunodeficiency syndrome (AIDS) patients suffering from HIV-wasting syndrome, a condition of undesired weight loss and concomitant malnutrition. In late 1992, Unlined received FDA approval to market dronabinol as a treatment for patients suffering from this form of anorexia.[23] Currently, Unimed is developing new formulations and delivery mechanisms for dronabinol (e.g., metered inhalant aerosol doses) that some patients might find more accommodating than smoked marijuana.

Supporters of allowing marijuana to be smoked for medicinal purposes were less than enthusiastic over the government's original approval and rescheduling of synthetic THC, even for treating such conditions as nausea and HIV-wasting syndrome. From their viewpoint, smoked marijuana offers superior pharmacological benefits over the drug's pill form, and the approval of oral THC had less to do with sanctioning a new cancer chemotherapy treatment than it did with maintaining the government's longstanding position that marijuana smoking, even for therapeutic purposes, is both harmful and illegal, and has no acceptable place in medical practice.

In July 1999, DEA issued a final rule transferring Marinol from Schedule II to Schedule III of the Controlled Substances Act.[24] The agency was responding to a 1995 petition from Unimed asking for a reconsideration of Marinol's scheduling. The petition sought only the rescheduling of the drug's prescription form and not tetrahydrocannabinol or natural marijuana, both of which will remain in Schedule I under the Act. The reclassification was granted after a review by DEA and the DHHS found that there was little evidence of illicit abuse of the drug. With the rescheduling, Marinol will be subject to the lesser regulatory controls and criminal sanctions of Schedule III. The action will also lift annual production quotas for the drug previously imposed under Schedule II.

---

[23] Two Drugs Approved for AIDS. *The Washington Post*, December 24, 1992. p. A5.

[24] U.S. Dept. of Justice. Drug Enforcement Administration. Schedules of Controlled Substances: Rescheduling of the Food and Drug Administration Approved Product Containing Synthetic Dronabinol [(-)-delta nine-(trans)-Tetrahydrocannabinol] in Sesame Oil and Encapsulated in Soft Gelatin Capsules From Schedule II to Schedule III. *Federal Register*, v. 64, no. 127, July 2, 1999. p. 35928.

PHS Ends Marijuana Treatment Use Program

For several years, under aegis of its investigational or "treatment use" policy, FDA allowed a limited number of seriously ill patients to use smoked marijuana for "compassionate" purposes.[25] The drug was grown by the federal government on its "marijuana farm" in Oxford, Mississippi.

On June 21, 1991, Public Health Service (PHS) officials announced that the marijuana treatment program would be phased out.[26] Among the reasons offered for the policy shift was that more patients than originally anticipated were seeking admission and that expansion of the treatment program might send a "bad signal" to the rest of the country. PHS officials explained that a continuation of the program could have been perceived as the government endorsing marijuana smoking as a form of medical therapy, a position that might weaken the administration's policy against the use of illegal drugs.

The program was officially terminated on March 9, 1992, when PHS officials announced that the government would continue to support participants currently in the program, but would no longer accept new applicants. Instead, they said the government would encourage patients wishing to apply for the treatment program to seek alternative means of medical therapy. In defending its position, PHS stated there was no scientific evidence that the drug was assisting patients, and issued a warning that using smoked marijuana as a form of medical therapy might be harmful to people with compromised immune systems (i.e., AIDS patients).[27]

SYNTHETIC VERSUS SMOKED MARIJUANA

Among the contentious issues in the medical marijuana debate, none is more central than the argument over whether smoked marijuana is therapeutically and pharmacologically superior to drugs made from synthetic THC like dronabinol (Marinol). Proponents, particularly those who back the use of natural marijuana, argue that the drug's primary active ingredient THC, can be more rapidly and

---

[25] Ray, *Drugs, Society, and Human Behavior*, p. 415. According to the authors, FDA's involvement in the use of marijuana as a medication began in 1975 following the outcome of a legal dispute over a patient's desire to smoke marijuana for treating glaucoma. As part of the resolution in the case, a limited program was started whereby the National Institute on Drug Abuse would provide medical-grade marijuana cigarettes to certain patients under an FDA-approved "compassionate use" protocol.

[26] Isikoff, Michael. HHS to Phase Out Marijuana Program. *The Washington Post*, June 22, 1991. p.A14.

[27] US Rescinds Approval of Marijuana as Therapy. *The New York Times*, March 11, 1992. p. A21.

efficiently absorbed via the lungs through smoking. They also maintain that by employing this route of administration, patients have better control over their dosage and can experience more rapid symptomatic relief.

However, some health experts and government officials argue to the contrary. They insist that people who smoke marijuana frequently are exposing themselves to a rather crude and potentially harmful drug delivery system. Moreover, they argue that the smoke from a burning marijuana cigarette contains a variety of toxic chemicals that could be harmful, especially to users whose medical condition might be compromised further by choosing to smoke the drug for self-treatment. Also, they maintain that there is little evidence, based on controlled clinical trial, that smoking marijuana offers patients any therapeutic advantages over a synthetic THC product like Marinol. As such, health officials advise that before patients insist on trying natural marijuana, they should first seek a doctor's prescription and start with the synthetic version of the drug.

MEDICAL USES OF MARIJUANA

The issue of smoking marijuana as a means of treating the symptoms associated with certain medical conditions has been debated for nearly 30 years. Starting with claims made in the early 1970s by some cancer and glaucoma patients that smoking marijuana could counter complications associated with their diseases, the number of therapeutic claims made for the drug has increased substantially. Today, the list of conditions that are allegedly treatable by smoking the drug has expanded to include pain, symptoms related to AIDS, and spasticity associated with various movement disorders.

Although historical accounts of marijuana's medicinal applications date back centuries, most reports are based on anecdotal rather than science-based clinical evaluations. However, beginning in the early 1970s, when marijuana was deemed by Congress to have "no currently accepted medical use" as a result of being placed in Schedule I of the Controlled Substance Act, both medical marijuana supporters and investigators began looking at whether the drug's ever-expanding list of claimed health benefits was supportable by scientific evidence. Trying to reach such determinative evidence has been problematic.

The information contained in this section of the report is excerpted from several sources that focus primarily on the medicinal uses for marijuana, and its oral-dose forms, most frequently cited by patients and covered in the medical literature. These uses typically include chemotherapy-related nausea treatment, appetite stimulation for HIV patients, movement disorders such as multiple sclerosis, glaucoma, and analgesia. The sources referenced include past and current scientific review articles, the National Institutes of Health's (NIH) 1997 *Workshop on the Medical Utility of Marjuana*,[28] and the Institutes of Medicine's (IOM) 1999 report *Marijuana and Medicine. Assessing the Science Base.*[29] In addition to being frequently cited, they provide a comprehensive evaluation of the scientific, social, and political issues involved.

Chemotherapy and Nausea Treatment

Research data published in the late 1970s suggested that oral marijuana - referring to the synthetic form of its psychoactive ingredient tetrahydrocannabinol (THC) - was effective in controlling nausea experienced by some cancer patients who were undergoing radiation and chemotherapy. Researchers Frytak and Moertel who reviewed major studies that had been conducted to characterize THC's role in cancer therapy concluded that:

> At the present time, it would appear that THC may have some clinical role as an antiemetic [anti-nauseal agent in teenagers or very young adults who have proved resistant to phenothiazines] – [phenothiazines are powerful neuropsychiatric drugs that can also be used to treat nausea] particularly those young patients who have previously found marijuana to be tolerable.] In cancer patients in the usual older age groups, THC cannot be recommended because a safe and effective dose has not yet been established. Regardless of age group, particular caution must be observed for possible serious adverse drug interactions that have not yet been clearly elucidated.[30]

Early clinical evaluations of marijuana were conducted primarily using oral dose synthetic THC rather than the smoked natural form of the drug. However, in an early placebo controlled study, published in the *Annals of Internal Medicine*, Chang and associates examined the efficacy of oral and smoked THC as an antiemetic and found that the smoked form of the drug was more reliable than the oral form in achieving blood concentration of THC necessary for therapeutic purposes. Chang also noted, however, that for some patients, especially

---

[28] Institutes of Health. *Workshop on the Medical Utility of Marijuana; a Report to the Director*, August 1997. [http://www.health.org/medmarj.htm], April 8, 1999.

[29] Institute of Medicine. *Marijuana and Medicine: Assessing the Science Base*. Washington, D.C., National Academy Press, 1999. [http://www.nap.edu/books/O3O9071550/html/] (Hereafter cited as IOM, Marijuana and Medicine: Assessing the Science Base)

[30] Frytak, Stephen, and Charles G. Moertel. Management of Nausea and Vomiting in the Cancer Patient. *Journal of the American Medical Association*, v. 245, January 23-30, 1981. p. 395.

nonsmokers, the inhalation of marijuana smoke was quite harsh and objectionable.[31] In a separate study published in the same journal issue, Frytak and colleagues, in referring to Chang's data, said one might conclude that the inhalation route for THC would be the most effective. They concluded, however, that although clinical studies showed oral THC to be effective in treating nausea associated with chemotherapy:

> the preparation of standardized THC [marijuana] cigarettes is quite tedious, and many patients would find this route unacceptable. Smoking the substance we know as marijuana (a combination of over 300 chemical agents, some inherently carcinogenic) would not be an acceptable substitute for THC either.[32]

In 1982, the Institute of Medicine of the National Academy of Sciences issued a report entitled *Marijuana and Health*. The report's executive summary made the following observations about marijuana's therapeutic potential:

> Preliminary studies suggest that marijuana and its derivatives or analogues might be useful in the treatment of the raised intraocular pressure of glaucoma, in the control of the severe nausea and vomiting caused by cancer chemotherapy, and in the treatment of asthma.[33]

However, the report added the following caution:

> in these and all other conditions, much more work is needed. Because marijuana and [oral] delta-9-THC often produce troublesome psychotropic or cardiovascular effects that limit their therapeutic usefulness, particularly in older patients, the greatest therapeutic potential probably lies in the use of synthetic analogues of marijuana derivatives with higher ratios of therapeutic to undesirable effects. [34]

A 1997 critique of marijuana's medicinal applications challenged the caliber of many of these earlier studies. In this often cited review article, Voth and Schwartz noted that most of the studies conducted to compare marijuana (THC) to

---

[31] Chang, A. E., et al. Delta-9-Tetrahydrocannabinol as an Antiemetic in Cancer Patients Receiving High-Dose Methotrexate: A Prospective Randomized Evaluation. *Annals of Internal* Medicine, v. 91, 1979. p. 823.

[32] Frytak, Stephen, et al. Delta-9-Tetrahydrocannabinol as an Antiemetic for Patients Receiving Cancer Chemotherapy: A Comparison with Prochlorperazine and a Placebo. *Annals of Internal Medicine*, v. 91, 1979. p. 830.

[33] Institute of Medicine. Division of Health Sciences Policy. *Marijuana and Health*. Washington, D.C., National Academy Press, 1982. p. 4.

[34] Ibid.

either another drug or a placebo in treating nausea experienced by patients undergoing chemotherapy, used oral THC rather than smoked marijuana.[35] They "found no pattern of THC efficacy for any type of tumor or chemotherapy," but concluded that oral TITIC doses "have been effective in treating nausea associated with cancer chemotherapy if patients are pretreated and doses are repeated every 3 to 6 hours for approximately 24 hours."[36] Additionally, the authors pointed out that "numerous safe and effective non-cannabinoids are available for the control of chemotherapy-associated nausea," and noted the importance of these alternatives "given the side effects found in studies of THC."[37]

In a similar type of review article, published in 1998 in the *Journal of the American Pharmaceutical Association*, Taylor noted that several studies have demonstrated that smoking marijuana is at least as effective as prochlorperazine - an anti-nausea drug.[38] He went on to say, however, that due to the availability of newer anti-nausea medications, the number of cancer physicians recommending illicit marijuana is now quite small. In commenting on a recent study measuring the effectiveness of intravenous ondansetron (Zofran) and dexamethasone, Taylor noted that the two drug combination produced a complete anti-emetic response in a vast majority of the patients. He cautioned, however, that these results also demonstrate that approximately 20% of cancer chemotherapy patients will not receive a full antiemetic response to ondansetron, and for this group, especially those with extreme retching, there are anecdotal reports that smoking marijuana may be a benefit.[39]

In 1997, the Ad Hoc Group of Experts[40] released its report entitled *Workshop on the Medical Utility of Marijuana*.[41] The report's executive summary recognized that "there is a large body of literature on the effects of cannabinoids on chemotherapy-induced nausea and vomiting," and reiterated the fact that "most of the clinical studies used oral dronabinol [synthetic THC] rather than smoked

[35] Voth, Eric A., and Richard H. Schwartz. Medicinal Applications of Delta-9- Tetrahydrocannabinol and Marijuana. *Annals of Internal Medicine*, v. 126, May 1997. (Hereafter cited as Voth, Medicinal Applications of Delta-9-Tetrahydrocannabinol)

[36] Ibid., p. 792.

[37] Ibid., p. 792.

[38] Taylor, H. Gordon. Analysis of the Medical Use of Marijuana and its Societal Implications. *Journal of the American PharmaceuticalAssociation*, v.38, March/April 1998. p. 220-227. (Hereafter cited as Taylor, Analysis of the Medical Use of Marijuana)

[39] Ibid., p. 224.

[40] The Ad Hoc Group of Experts was an NIH appointed team of doctors and scientists who conducted a 2-day scientific workshop on the medical use of marijuana. The public meeting was held February 19-20, 1997.

[41] National Institutes of Health. The Ad Hoc Group of Experts. *Workshop on the Medical Utility of Marijuana, Report to the Director*, August 1997. (Hereafter cited as National Institutes of Health, *Workshop on the Medical Utility of Marijuana*)

marijuana."[42] The Expert Group also reconfirmed the point that "since the approval of dronabinol in the mid-1980s for the relief of nausea and vomiting associated with cancer chemotherapy, more effective antiemetics have been developed, such as ondansetron, granisetron, and dolasetron, each combined with dexamethasone."[43] According to the Expert Group, "the relative efficacy of cannabinoids versus these newer antiemetics has not been evaluated."[44] Their summary concluded by noting that it is still unknown whether smoked marijuana would benefit patients who do not respond to these newer anti-nausea drugs.

In its 1999 report, *Marijuana and Medicine. Assessing the Science Base*, the Institute of Medicine (IOM) pointed out that the mechanism by which chemotherapy induces vomiting is not completely understood. The report gives a description of the qualities anti-emetic drugs should have that would be most advantageous to patients, and speculates that most chemotherapy patients would probably not want to use marijuana or THC for nausea control. It noted that the psychoactive chemicals in marijuana are "mildly effective in preventing emesis in some patients receiving cancer chemotherapy," but that there are pharmaceutical preparations available today that are more effective.[45] IOM also observed, however, that "until the development of rapid-onset antiemetic drug delivery systems, there will likely remain a subpopulation of patients for whom standard antiemetic therapy is ineffective and who suffer from debilitating emesis."[46] It stated further that for some of these patients, the harmful effects of smoking marijuana for a short period of time might be outweighed by the drug's antinausea benefits, especially in those who suffer from severe nausea which cannot be controlled by traditional medication. The IOM recommends that these patients should be evaluated, on a case-by-ease basis, and treated under close medical supervision.[47]

Appetite Stimulation

According to Voth and Schwartz, "the literature contains few studies with objective data on the use of either pure THC or crude marijuana for appetite stimulation."[48] Without speculating on whether smoking marijuana can act as an

---

[42] Ibid., p. 3.
[43] Ibid., p. 3.
[44] Ibid., p. 3.
[45] IOM, *Marijuana and Medicine. Assessing the Science Base*, p. 148.
[46] Ibid., p. 154.
[47] Ibid., p. 154.
[48] Voth, *Medicinal Applications of Delta-9-Tetrahydrocannabinol*, p. 793.

effective appetite stimulant, the authors allowed that, "the appetite-stimulating effect of THC [orally administered] may be beneficial for patients with wasting related to the acquired immunodeficiency syndrome (AIDS) and those with severe cancer related anorexia."[49] However, after noting the beneficial relationship between the use of oral dronabinol and wasting syndrome, they pointed out that "this issue is complex because appetite stimulation is a surrogate measure for useful weight maintenance or gain and for effective calorie intake, which are far more important measures than appetite alone."[50]

In his review article, Taylor acknowledged that AIDS patients "commonly smoke marijuana to relieve the nausea caused by antiretroviral drugs and for weight gain."[51] He also agreed that there are numerous anecdotal reports of marijuana's superiority over oral dronabinol in treating weight loss, and that AIDS patients report that smoking it makes them feel better in general. Taylor warned, however, that because of their compromised immune systems, AIDS patients are more susceptible to possible bacteriological contaminants that may be in marijuana. He also noted that because "smoking drugs does increase the risk of *Pneumocystis carinji* and bacterial pneumonias in HIV-positive patients," they are more at risk for the consequences of marijuana-induced injury to their immune systems.[52] Commenting on the issue of whether smoking marijuana can increase the viral load on AIDS patients, Taylor reported that there is no confirmatory evidence to support this hypothesis, and emphasized that "one study found no indication that psychoactive drugs, including marijuana, accelerate the progression of AIDS."[53]

The report from the Expert Group reached essentially the same conclusions, agreeing that studies and survey data in health populations "have shown a strong relationship between marijuana use and increased food intake."[54] However, it also acknowledged that there have been no controlled studies of marijuana in the AIDS-wasting syndrome, nor any systematic studies of the drug's effects on immunological status in HIV-infected patients.[55] The Expert Group also cautioned that smoking [tobacco, marijuana, or crack cocaine] drugs in general has been shown to increase the risk of developing bacterial pneumonia in HIV-positive immune-compromised patients.

---

[49] Ibid., p. 793.
[50] Ibid., p. 793.
[51] Taylor, *Analysis of the Medical Use of Marijuana*, p. 224.
[52] Ibid., p. 224.
[53] Ibid., p. 224.
[54] National Institutes of Health, *Workshop on the Medical Utility of Marijuana*, p. 4.
[55] Ibid., p. 4.

IOM's recent characterization of marijuana's use in the treatment of malnutrition and wasting syndrome differed little from the previous reports. It noted that the use of cannabinoids to stimulate appetite and increase weight gain has only been clinically evaluated in trials that used oral synthetic THC rather smoked marijuana. IOM called attention to the fact that malnutrition and weight loss can be treated with the prescription drug megestrol acetate. Sold under the brand name Megace, this appetite stimulant was approved in 1993, and is considered to be more effective than dronabinol in inducing weight gain.[56] IOM stated that although controlled laboratory studies on normal, healthy adults have shown that smoked marijuana can increase appetite, food intake, and body weight, to date, there have been no controlled investigations to determine whether the drug has the same positive effect in HIV patients.[57] According to IOM, a clinical trial of this type is currently underway.

Movement Disorders

The reviews referred to in this report reached similar conclusions regarding the use of marijuana in treating a variety of neurological and movement disorders. They stipulated, for the most part, that several anecdotal and a few case studies have been reported attesting to the drug's role in relieving spasticity associated with multiple sclerosis (MS). Voth reported, however, that in one well-controlled study of the effects of smoking marijuana in MS patients, their "posture and balance were negatively affected by the treatment and were actually worse than at baseline."[58]

In addressing marijuana's place in the treatment of other neurological disorders, the Expert Group said that there was evidence from animal studies to suggest a possible role for cannabinoids in the treatment of certain types of epileptic seizures. They qualified this hypothesis, however, by noting that there is little information on the use of the drug for the actual treatment of epilepsy. In addition, the Expert Group reported that neither smoked marijuana nor oral THC has proven effective in treating Parkinson's disease or Huntington's chorea.[59]

IOM uses the expression "movement disorders" to describe a broad group of neurological complications that affect the brain, spinal cord, or peripheral nerves and muscles. In the case of multiple sclerosis, IOM acknowledged that marijuana

---

[56] IOM, *Marijuana and Medicine: Assessing the Science Base*, p. 156.
[57] Ibid., p. 156.
[58] Voth, *Medicinal Applications of Delta-9-Tetrahydrocannabinol*, p. 794.
[59] National Institutes of Health, *Workshop on the Medical Utility of Marijuana*, p. 3.

is frequently reported to reduce the muscle spasticity associated with the disease, but then it noted that these abundant anecdotal reports are not well-supported by clinical data.[60] In addition, IOM said that, due to a lack of good animal models to study spasticity in MS, there is virtually "no supporting animal data to encourage clinical research."[61] Regardless, the report encouraged the investigation of the drug for potential use in MS therapy.

According to the IOM report, the use of smoked marijuana to treat other movement disorders appears to be even less encouraging. After surveying the literature for evidence of marijuana's effectiveness in treating such movement disorders as dystonia (abnormal tension in bodily tissue), Huntington's Disease, Parkinson's Disease, and Tourettes Syndrome, the IOM concluded that although there are a few isolated reports of individuals with such disorders benefitting from marijuana, there are, as yet, no published surveys indicating that most patients gain any significant relief from using the drug.[62] IOM also noted that "with the exception of multiple sclerosis, the evidence to recommend clinical trials of cannabinoids in movement disorders is relatively weak."[63]

Glaucoma

All sources agreed that cannabinoids can lower the intraocular pressure (IOP) associated with glaucoma in humans. Voth pointed out, however, that even though THC is beneficial for the treatment of glaucoma, "no evidence indicates that either pure THC or crude marijuana affects or arrests the underlying disease."[64] Taylor also acknowledged that marijuana has therapeutic potential, but emphasized that because THC cannot penetrate into the coruea, glaucoma is best treated with ophthalmic drops.[65] In contrast, the Expert Group, contended that a topical dose of THC had been developed, but that it turned out to be ineffective in lowering intraocular pressure.[66]

IOM confirmed that cannabinoids or marijuana can reduce lOP when administered orally, intravenously, or by inhalation, but not when administered topically. Furthermore, it stated that even though evidence shows that a reduction in lOP by medications or surgery can slow the rate of glaucoma progression,

---

[60] IOM, *Marijuana and Medicine. Assessing the Science Base*, p. 161.
[61] Ibid., p. 161.
[62] Ibid., p. 169.
[63] Ibid., p. 170.
[64] Voth, *Medicinal Applications of Delta-9- Tetrahydrocannabinol*, p. 794.
[65] Taylor, *Analysis of the Medical Use of Marijuana*, p. 224.
[66] National Institutes of Health, *Workshop on the Medical Utility of Marijuana*, p. 4.

"there is no direct evidence to support the benefits of cannabinoids or marijuana on the natural progression of glaucoma, visual acuity, or optic atrophy."[67]

Analgesia

Voth discussed the use of marijuana for analgesia or pain relief only in the context of a handful of illnesses [e.g., headache, dysentery, menstrual cramps, and depression] that are often cited by marijuana advocates as medical reasons to justify the drug being available as a prescription medication.[68] As such, he does not address specifically whether oral or smoked marijuana possesses any pain relieving qualities.

The Expert Group reported that no clinical trials have been conducted to examine the impact of smoked marijuana in patients with naturally occurring pain. However, they did identify two controlled clinical studies of cancer pain comparing graded doses of oral delta-9-THC to placebo, one of which included graded doses of codeine as a control. The Group reported that studies indeed showed an analgesic effect, but that the therapeutic margin between doses that produced useful analgesia, and those that produced unacceptable central nervous system effects, was quite narrow.[69] Taylor's findings were in virtual agreement with the Expert Group. He acknowledged that marijuana has been used for centuries to relieve pain, but that scientifically controlled studies confirming this use are almost nonexistent.[70]

IOM reviewed studies conducted to assess marijuana's pain-relieving capacity and found that although clinical trials have been few, "data from animal studies indicate that cannabinoids could be useful analgesics."[71] Where clinical evaluations were conducted, notably in studies where pain was experimentally-induced, consistent analgesia was not demonstrated. Several methodological flaws were noted in these studies. However, in studies it considered methodologically sound, IOM concluded that the most encouraging clinical data came from cancer studies where the analgesic effects of cannabinoids compared favorably with a weak analgesic such as codeine.

In pain associated with minor surgical procedures, IOM found no analgesic effect of THC, and where marijuana smoking was used for treating migraine

---

[67] IOM, *Marijuana and Medicine: Assessing the Science Base*, p. 175.
[68] Voth, *Medicinal Applications of Delta-9-Tetrahydrocannabinol*, p. 795.
[69] National Institutes of Health, *Workshop on the Medical Utility of Marijuana*, p. 2.
[70] Taylor, *Analysis of the Medical Use of Marijuana*, p. 224.
[71] IOM, *Marijuana and Medicine: Assessing the Science Base*, p. 140.

headaches, they found no conclusive clinical data to support the drug's use. Despite the inherent limitations in some studies reviewed, IOM concluded that evidence from animal and human studies suggest that cannabinoids "can produce a significant analgesic effect," but that the effect's magnitude and whether it can be maintained over time, needed to be addressed in future studies.[72]

Summary of Findings of the Medical Literature

These summaries of the literature on medical marijuana made an effort to assess the scientific validity behind the many therapeutic claims made for the drug. Although the evaluations review essentially the same published scientific literature, and agreed on several scientific points, there was a lack of consensus on the interpretation of the data. Voth, for instance, acknowledged that oral [synthetic] THC is useful in treating patients with chemotherapy-induced nausea or AIDS-associated wasting syndrome. Furthermore, he predicted that if newer and more refined delivery mechanisms are ever developed for THC, the drug may achieve even wider acceptance in medical practice. However, on the issue of whether smoked marijuana has medicinal value, Voth was adamant that "crude marijuana does not qualify as a medicine," and should remain a Schedule I drug.[73]

Taylor, on the other hand, offers a somewhat different point of view. He agrees with Voth in noting the risks associated with chronic marijuana smoking: toxicity to the lungs, potential exposure to certain disease-producing contaminants, and possible impairment of the immune system. Unlike Voth, however, he makes less of an issue over whether the evidence for or against marijuana's medical use is based on controlled studies using the oral or the smoked form of the drug, and states that from his perspective, "marijuana clearly benefits patients with intractable pain, neurological disorders, nausea and vomiting, and glaucoma."[74] Taylor speculates further that marijuana's mechanism of action is probably different from those of drugs typically used to treat these conditions, and may, therefore have adjunctive value.[75]

Based on their reviews of contemporary studies conducted to address marijuana's therapeutic potential, both the Expert Group and IOM concluded that further scientific research is needed. They stressed that many of the answers in the ongoing scientific and medical debate over the safe and effective use of

---

[72] Ibid., p. 145.
[73] Voth, *Medicinal Applications of Delta-9-Tetrahydrocannabinol*, p. 796.
[74] Taylor, *Analysis of the Medical Use of Marijuana*, p. 226.
[75] Ibid., p. 226.

marijuana, or its synthetic analogues, will be forthcoming only through additional well-controlled clinical investigations. The Expert Group advised that researchers give consideration to the full range of potential questions that could be addressed, propose ways to address the most important of these, and design their study protocols accordingly.[76] Adopting this strategy, they felt, might enhance the possibility of gaining funding support from federal agencies.

The IOM also offered several recommendations relating to future studies of marijuana and cannabinoid drugs. It acknowledged that completed scientific studies support the therapeutic potential of cannabinoids in the treatment of certain medical conditions, but also pointed out that the drug's therapeutic value is probably influenced significantly by its psychological effects. According to the Institute, these effects can be subjective and either influence symptoms in a way that might create false impressions, or be interpreted as a beneficial form of adjunctive therapy.[77] IOM further cautioned that because marijuana is a crude TUG delivery system capable of delivering other harmful substances, smoked marijuana should generally not be recommended for medical use.

With this thought in mind, the Institute predicted that if there is any future for the drug as a medicine, it will come from its isolated cannabinoids and their synthetic derivatives. It further stated that because isolated cannabinoids can provide more reliable effects than crude plant mixtures, the purpose of clinical trial using smoked marijuana should not be the development of marijuana as a licensed drug.[78] In order to gain a better understanding of the health risks associated with smoking marijuana, including further insight into its medical legitimacy, IOM recommended the following:

- Research should continue into the physiological effects of synthetic and plant-derived cannabinoids and the natural function of cannabinoids found in the body. Because cannabinoids have different effects in the body, research should include, but not be restricted to, effects attributable to THC alone.

- Clinical trials of cannabinoid drugs for symptom management should be conducted with the goal of developing rapid-onset, reliable, and safe delivery systems.

---

[76] National Institutes of Health, *Workshop on the Medical Utility of Marijuana*, p. 38.
[77] IOM, *Marijuana and Medicine: Assessing the Science Base*, p. 10
[78] Ibid., p. II.

- Psychological effects of cannabinoids such as anxiety reduction and sedationwhich can influence perceived medical benefits - should be evaluated in clinical trials.

- Studies to define the individual health risks of smoking marijuana should be conducted, especially in populations where use is prevalent.

- Clinical trials of marijuana use for medical purposes should be conducted under the following limited circumstances: trials should involve only short-term marijuana use (6 months or less); be conducted in patients with conditions for which there is a reasonable expectation of effectiveness; be approved by an Institutional Review Board (IRB); collect data about efficacy.

- Short-term use of smoked marijuana (6 months or less) for patients with debilitating symptoms must meet the following conditions: failure of all approved drugs to provide relief has been documented; the symptoms can reasonably be expected to be relieved by rapid-onset cannabinoid drugs; treatment is administered under medical supervision in a manner that allows assessment of treatment effectiveness; and research involves an IRB-like process that can provide guidance within 24 hours of a physician's request to provide marijuana for a specified use.

CURRENT RESEARCH ON MEDICAL MARIJUANA

In response to IOM's recommendations, the Department of Health and Human Services (DHHS), on May 21, 1999, announced new policies and procedures for obtaining research-grade marijuana for purposes of conducting scientifically valid clinical investigations using the drug.[79] The marijuana provided is available not only for NIH-supported studies, but for research funded by other sources as well. According to DHHS, an ad-hoc Public Health Service committee reviews non-NIH-funded clinical studies to determine if they are designed in a way that will produce the kind of safety and efficacy data needed to meet FDA's drug approval standards. Researchers who want to investigate the potential therapeutic effects of smoking marijuana have to file an Investigational New Drug application with the FDA and be properly registered with the DEA for using a Schedule I substance.

---

[79] U.S. Dept. of Health and Human Services. Fact Sheet. Investigating Possible Medical Uses of Marijuana. May 21,1999. [http://www.hhs.gov/news/press/1999pres/990521.html]

While it has become a bit easier in recent years to obtain research-grade marijuana to conduct clinical studies, the number of clinical investigators involved in federally supported studies of the drug's therapeutic potential is quite small. According to the National Institute on Drug Abuse (NIDA), the National Institutes of Health is currently supporting only one research project looking at the medical benefits of smoked marijuana. Under the direction of Dr. Margaret Haney at the New York State Psychiatric Institute, the study is measuring the effects of THC and marijuana in individuals with HIV/AIDS. The purpose of the study, which is cofunded by NIDA and the National Center for Complementary and Alternative Medicine, is to compare the effects of smoked marijuana and oral THC in HIV patients with unintended weight loss. In addition to analyzing food intake and body composition, the researchers are measuring mood, physical symptoms (e.g., nausea, stomach pain), psychomotor task performance, and sleep in order to assess the specificity of drug effects on food intake in relation to other behaviors. Funded for $1,341,926 over 3 years, with an estimated funding level of $496,454 for FY2002, the study is expected to be completed in June 2003.

In another study, supported by several NIH Institutes and recently completed, Dr. Donald Abrams at the University of California, San Francisco, conducted a randomized prospective study to assess the short-term effects of smoked marijuana and oral THC on the metabolism of protease inhibitors (the latest-generation AIDS drug), the immune system, and the level of HIV- 1 viral load in persons with HIV- 1 infection. The study also measured changes in weight gain or in appetite. Study participants received either NIDA supplied marijuana cigarettes, an oral tablet of THC, or placebo capsules. A preliminary report on the study at the World AIDS Conference reported that patients with HIV infection taking protease inhibitors did not experience short-term adverse virologic effects for using cannabinoids, either oral or smoked. The results of the Abrams study have yet to be published.

MEDICAL MARIJUANA: STATE BALLOT INITIATIVES

During the past 5 years, voters at the state level have agreed to a variety of initiatives that allow patients to smoke marijuana for medical purposes. In 1996, after lengthy and contentious petition drives waged chiefly by active supporters of the drug's medical use, citizens in California and Arizona passed referendums making marijuana legally available for therapeutic purposes.[80]

With the 1998 election the list grew as medical marijuana referendums were considered by voters in several other states.[81] Initiatives were passed in Alaska, Arizona (for the second time), the District of Columbia, Nevada, Oregon, and Washington. In addition, voters in Colorado adopted Amendment 19, allowing for the medical use of marijuana. The amendment was later invalidated, however, when Colorado's Secretary of State ruled that its backers had not collected the required number of signatures. When legal challenges and subsequent recounts determined that the number of signatures had been sufficient, the Colorado Supreme Court ordered that the amendment be placed on the ballot for 2000, where it passed handily.

In the District of Columbia, residents voted on Initiative 59, a referendum that would have permitted the possession, use, cultivation and distribution of marijuana if recommended by a physician for serious illness. However, the results were not tabulated and released right away due to an amendment attached to the District's FY1999 appropriation bill[82] that barred spending any money to tally the initiative's final vote count. The amendment, sponsored by Representative Robert Barr, was eventually challenged in U.S. District Court, and on September 17, 1999, U.S. District Judge Richard Roberts held that the so-called "Barr Amendment" did not preclude the D.C. Board of Elections and Ethics from counting, announcing or certifying the results of the referendum.[83] When the results were finally released, Initiative 59 had passed with 69% of the vote.[84]

Despite the Judge's ruling, it is unlikely that patients in the District of Columbia will be able to smoke marijuana for medicinal purposes anytime soon. The reason is that during consideration of the District's FY2000 budget, the 106th Congress agreed to an amendment blocking any effort to reduce penalties associated with the possession, use, or distribution of any Schedule I controlled drug or any tetrahydrocannabinol (marijuana) derivative. Going even further, the amendment said that "the Legalization of Marijuana for Medical Treatment

---

[80] During the 1996 election, the marijuana ballot initiatives under consideration were Proposition 215 in California; Proposition 200 in Arizona.

[81] The information on state medical marijuana referendums was excerpted from the following websites: [http://www.lindesmith.org/news/election2.html], [http ://norml.orglmedical!pets98. htmlj, and [http://www.levellers.org/election98.html].

[82] P.L. 105-277, Section 171: Omnibus Consolidated and Emergency Supplemental Appropriation Act, 1999.

[83] Wayne Turner, et al. v. District of Columbia Bd. Of Elections and Ethics, Civ. Action No. 98-2634(RWR), (D.C.D.C. Sept. 17, 1999), 1999 U.S. Dist. LEXIS 16595.

[84] Miller, Bill, and Spencer S. Hsu. Results Are Out: Marijuana Initiative Passes. The Washington Post. September 21, 1999. p. Al.

Initiative of 1998, also known as Initiative 59, approved by the electors of the District of Columbia on November 3, 1998, shall not take effect."[85] This same restrictive language has been included in the District of Columbia's FY2001 and FY2002 appropriations bills (see discussion of the medical marijuana legislation introduced in the 106th Congress).

In 1999, voters in Maine agreed to a referendum allowing doctors to prescribe marijuana for patients with specified debilitating conditions. In the 2000 election, marijuana initiatives were back on the ballot once again. Voters in Colorado adopted their medical marijuana amendment for the second time, while citizens in Nevada passed the same marijuana question they had considered back in 1998.[86] Besides the election referendums, the state legislature m Hawaii became the first to approve the use of marijuana for certain medical conditions.[87] To date, with the exception of the District of Columbia, whose medical marijuana initiative has been stymied by Congress, the following states have adopted referendums or legislation (Hawaii) allowing patients to smoke marijuana for therapeutic purposes:

Alaska: Measure 8 - Passed in 1998, the measure lets patients suffering from debilitating medical conditions possess up to 1 ounce of marijuana or three mature plants for medicinal use. It directs the state to create a confidential registry of patients entitled to use marijuana for medicinal purposes under the Act. The measure exempts physicians from prosecution under state law for advising patients about marijuana's medical benefits.

Arizona: Proposition 200 - The 1996 referendum would have allowed Arizona physicians to prescribe any Schedule I controlled substance (i.e., marijuana, heroin, LSD, etc.) to treat disease or relieve the pain and suffering of seriously or terminally ill patients. However, when the referendum was adopted, the state legislature stepped in and passed a law that said that Schedule I drugs (like marijuana) could be prescribed by doctors only if they were approved by FDA and authorized by the U.S. Congress first. In the 1998 election, voters considered Proposition 300, which, if passed, would have allowed the state legislature's medical marijuana bill to become law. In the end, Proposition 300 was defeated, allowing Arizona doctors to prescribe Schedule I controlled drugs under the terms of the original Proposition 200.

California: Proposition 215 - Called the Compassionate Use Act of 1996, the proposition ensures that seriously ill Californians have the right to obtain and use

---

[85] P.L. 106-113, Section 167: Consolidated Appropriation Act, FY2000.
[86] Under Nevada law, an initiative must be approved in two consecutive general elections before it becomes law.
[87] Act 228, Session Laws 2000.

marijuana for medical purposes. The medical use of the drug must be deemed appropriate and recommended by a physician who has determined that the patient's health would benefit from the use of marijuana. Patients and primary caregivers who use marijuana for medical purposes are not subject to criminal prosecution. Also, the proposition encouraged federal and state governments to implement a plan to provide for the drug's safe and affordable distribution for patients in need.

Colorado: Amendment 20 - Adopted in 2000, the amendment allows patients diagnosed with a serious or chronic illness and their caregivers to legally possess up to two ounces of marijuana for medical purposes. It also lets doctors provide seriously or chronically ill patients a written statement that they might benefit from the medical use of marijuana. Lastly, it establishes a confidential registry of patients and their caregivers who are allowed to possess marijuana for medicinal purposes.

Hawaii: Act 228 - Hawaii is the only state where the medical use of marijuana has been sanctioned through the legislative process rather than the ballot box. Signed into law in 2000, the legislation's stated purpose is "to ensure that seriously ill people are

not penalized by the State for the use of marijuana for strictly medical purposes when the patient's treating physician provides a professional opinion that the benefits of medical marijuana would likely outweigh the health risks for qualifying patient." The statute also allows qualifying patients and primary caregivers to assert the medical use of marijuana as an affirmative defense against any prosecution involving use of the drug for medical purposes.

Maine: Initiative Question 2 - Agreed to in 1999, the question amends Maine law and lets patients diagnosed with certain debilitating conditions use marijuana for medical purposes when a doctor determines that the use might be beneficial. It limits the amount of marijuana a patient can possess, and allows a legally designated person to assist in using the drug. Medical marijuana use is permitted by persons under age 18 if written consent is obtained from a parent or guardian. The drug may not be used for medicinal purposes in a public place or in a workplace.

Nevada: Ballot Question No. 9 - Passed in 1998, the question amended the state's constitution allowing patients, upon the advice of a doctor, to use marijuana for the treatment or alleviation of cancer, glaucoma, AIDS, nausea, epilepsy, and various disorders characterized by muscular spasticity. The amount of marijuana patients may possess or cultivate is not specified. In Nevada, before a ballot question can become law it must voted on and passed in consecutive elections. Question 9 passed again in year 2000.

Oregon: Measure 67 - Adopted in 1998, the measure allows patients with debilitating medical conditions to possess up to 3 ounces of marijuana, or to grow three plants for medicinal purposes, and directs the state to set up a system of registry identification cards for persons who meet the terms of the Act. The measure exempts persons engaged in the medical use of marijuana from the state's criminal laws for possession, delivery, or production of the drug. Also, the measure prohibits the possession, production, or delivery of marijuana for purposes not authorized by the provision.

Washington: Initiative 692 - Passed in 1998, the initiative allows patients with terminal or debilitating illnesses to possess up to a 60-day supply of marijuana for medical use. It says that physicians shall not be penalized for advising patients about the benefits of medical marijuana. It also says that nothing in the initiative supersedes the state's law prohibiting the acquisition, possession, manufacture, sale, or use of marijuana for non-medical purposes.

When the medical marijuana ballot initiatives were adopted in California and Arizona in 1996, the White House's Office of National Drug Control Policy (ONDCP) published a notice in the *Federal Register* calling the propositions a threat to the National Drug Control Strategy goal of reducing drug abuse in the United States.[88] Amplifying the Department of Justice's (DOJ) position further, the response stated that physicians would face legal sanction, including possible revocations of their DEA registrations, and exclusion from participating in Medicare and Medicaid programs, if they recommended or prescribed Schedule I controlled substances like marijuana.

In response, a group of California physicians and patients on January 14, 1997 filed a class-action suit contending that the government's threat to prosecute physicians who recommend the medical use of marijuana under the Compassionate Use Act of 1996 infringed on their First Amendment rights and interfered with the doctor-patient relationship.[89] Faced with the lawsuit, the Justice Department tempered its position and advised physicians that they were free to discuss with patients the risks and benefits of using marijuana for medicinal purposes.[90]

After several more states adopted medical marijuana initiatives during the 1998 elections, however, ONDCP released a policy statement regarding the

---

[88] U.S. Office of National Drug Control Policy. Administration Response to Arizona Proposition 200 and California Proposition 215. *Federal Register*, v. 62, no. 28, February 11, 1997. p.6164.

[89] Dr. Marcus Conant, ET AL., Plaintiffs, v. Barry R. McCaffrey, as Director, United States Office of National Drug Control Policy, ET AL., Defendants.

[90] Suro, Robert. U.S. Backs Off on Doctor-Patient Marijuana Discussions. *The Washington Post*, March 2, 1997. p. A14.

outcome of the referenda. The statement said, in essence, that even though the voters had agreed to referenda that would allow for the cultivation, possession, distribution, and consumption of marijuana for medical purposes under state or local law, the results of the referenda would not in any way alter marijuana's illegal status under federal law.

The statement added that even though the medical-scientific process in the United States had not closed the door on marijuana or any other substance that might offer potential therapeutic benefits, both law and common sense dictate that the process for establishing a substance as medicine should be thorough and science-based. The drug control policy office said that clinical data should be analyzed by experts in the FDA and the NIH for safety and efficacy, and if the scientific evidence demonstrates that the benefits of a substance outweigh its associated risks, the substance could be approved for medical use. According to ONDCP, this rigorous process protects public health, and allowing marijuana, or any other drug, to bypass the process would be unwise.

MEDICAL MARIJUANA: CANADA

In 2001, Canada become the first government to institute regulations giving citizens the legal right to possess and use marijuana for treating serious illnesses. According to Health Canada Online - the country's Website for health care information - patients can apply for an official authorization to possess marijuana for medicinal use if they fall into one of three categories: Category One - applicants who are terminally ill with a prognosis of less than 12 months to live; Category Two -patients with certain serious medical conditions such as multiple sclerosis, spinal cord injury, cancer, AID S/HIV infection, epilepsy; and Category Three - patients who have a serious medical condition that is unresponsive to conventional therapies.[91]

The medical marijuana program is regulated by Health Canada's Office of Cannabis Medical Access (OCMA). Under its rules, patients who qualify to participate in the program must apply to OCMA for official authorization to possess the drug. Applicants must provide information about their medical condition, whether they plan to grow their own supply of marijuana or obtain it from a dealer licensed by Health Canada. They must also include a written

---

[91] Health Canada Online. Marijuana for Medical Purposes, [http://www.hc-sc.gc.ca/english/ protection/marijuana.html]

statement from a medical specialist verifying that all other conventional treatments have been tried.

The marijuana provided under the Canadian medical marijuana program is being grown under a 5-year, $5.7 million contract with Prairie Plant Systems Inc. of Saskatoon, Saskatchewan.[92] According to the company's Website, under the terms of the contract, Prairie Plant Systems Inc. will be responsible for cultivating and drying the plants; conducting laboratory analysis; fabricating and storing the marijuana cigarettes and bulk material; and distributing the product to recipients authorized by Health Canada.[93] The company is scheduled to make its first delivery of medicinal-grade marijuana in January 2002. It will also be supplying the drug for a variety of research projects currently being supported by Health Canada as well. According to the OCMA, currently there are 753 persons taking part in Canada's medical marijuana program: 640 exemptees under its Section 56 regulations,[94] and another 113 persons given authorization to posses the drug under its more recent 2001 regulations.

MEDICAL MARIJUANA: THE U.S. SUPREME COURT

In April 1997, federal district court Judge Fern Smith, in a class action lawsuit, issued a preliminary injunction which prohibited government officials from threatening or prosecuting physicians, revoking their licenses, or excluding them from Medicare/Medicaid participation based upon conduct relating to medical marijuana that did not rise to the level of a criminal offense.[95] In her opinion, the district judge concluded that although the use of marijuana may be illegal, the First Amendment allows physicians to discuss and advocate its use for medical purposes. The suit was finally resolved when Judge William Alsup of the U.S. District Court for the Northern District of California ruled in September 2000 that the government exceeded its statutory authority when it threatened to revoke doctors' DEA registrations under the Controlled Substances Act (CSA). Under the judge's ruling, the government was permanently enjoined from

---

[92] Canadian Government Will Regulate Medical Marijuana Use Via Central Office. *Washington Fax*, August 9, 2001.

[93] Prairie Plant Systems Inc. [http://www.prairieplant.com/n.htm]

[94] Section 56 regulations refer to Section 56 of Canada's *Controlled Drugs and Substances Act*. Under the provision, Canada's Minister of Health may exempt any person, class of persons, or any controlled substance from the Act if the exemption is necessary for a medical or scientific purpose. It was this exemption which allowed persons to possess marijuana for medicinal use before the current policy and regulations were adopted in 2001.

[95] *Conant v. McCaffrey*, No. C 97-0139 FMS, 1997 U.S. Dist. LEXIS 8749 (N.D. CAL. April 30, 1997).

revoking a DEA registration merely because the doctor recommended medical marijuana to a patient based on a sincere medical judgement, and from starting any investigation solely for that reason.[96]

A separate legal conflict over medical marijuana involved the sale and distribution of the drug by several buyers clubs or cooperatives in California doing business under the aegis of the state's 1996 Compassionate Use Act, better known as Proposition 215. Some of the co-ops, including the Oakland Cannabis Buyers' Cooperative (OCBC), had been operating for years before the act was passed. The U.S. Justice Department charged that the centers, including the OCBC, were operating in violation of federal drug distribution laws, and in January 1998 filed a civil suit to have them shut down.[97]

In May 1998, the U.S. District Court for the Northern District of California issued a preliminary injunction ordering the centers closed. In the injunction, the court said that the distribution of marijuana by certain clubs and their agents was a probable violation of the Controlled Substances Act. Despite the district court's ruling, the Oakland Cooperative continued to make the drug available. The court found the Cooperative in contempt, rejecting the club's argument that they should be considered exempt from the CSA's prohibition against the distribution of marijuana because the distribution was "medically necessary."[98]

When the court rejected the club's argument, the OCBC filed a motion asking the district judge to modify the injunction so that marijuana could continue to be distributed to patients whose physicians would certify that use of the drug was a medical necessity. The court denied the motion, accepting the government's position that the court lacked the authority to grant the modification. The Cooperative then appealed the district court's ruling to the U.S. Court of Appeals for the Ninth Circuit.[99] In September 1999, the court of appeals reversed the district court, saying that by summarily denying the Cooperative's request for a modification, the lower court had failed to undertake the required analysis.[100]

The appellate court remanded the matter back to the district court and instructed it to reconsider the request for a modification that would, under the

---

[96] *Conant v. McCaffrey*, No. C 97-00139 WHA, 2000 U.S. Dist. LEXIS 13024 (ND. CAL. Sept. 8, 2000).

[97] *U.S. v. Cannabis Cultivators Club*, 5 F. Supp. 2d. 1086 (N.D. Cal. 1998).

[98] Id., In addition, in February 1999, the district court granted the government's motion to dismiss and rejected the Cannabis Cultivator's Club claim that the cooperative had a fundamental right to be free from the government's lawful exercise of its police powers.

[99] The Cooperative appealed both the contempt order and the denial of the Cooperative's motion to modify. The appeal of the contempt order became moot when the Cooperative promised to comply with the initial preliminary injunction.

[100] *U.S. v. Oakland Cannabis Buyers' Cooperative*, 109 F. 3d 1109 (9th Cir. 1999).

injunction, allow cannabis to be distributed to seriously ill individuals who need it for medical purposes. According to the Court of Appeals, the medical necessity defense was a defense that would likely apply in the circumstances.[101] The appellate court further instructed the district court to consider criteria for a medical necessity exemption, and, should it modify the injunction, to set forth the criteria in the modification order. On July 17, 2000, the district court, in an amended preliminary injunction, ruled that the defendants were enjoined from manufacturing or distributing marijuana under the GSA. The court granted the Cooperative's motion to modify the injunction to incorporate a medical necessity defense. Therefore, the injunction would not apply to patients who suffer from serious medical conditions and meet the criteria set forth in the injunction.[102]

When this ruling was issued, the Justice Department asked the U.S. Supreme Court to overturn the "medical necessity" defense for marijuana distribution. At the same time, it appealed the ruling from the Ninth Circuit Court that had allowed the Oakland buyers' club to provide marijuana to patients with serious medical conditions. In August 2000, the U.S. Supreme Court granted the Department's request to stop the Cooperative from distributing marijuana.[103] Because the decision raised significant questions about the ability of the federal government to enforce the nation's drug laws, the Supreme Court agreed in November to hear arguments in the medical necessity case.[104]

On May 14, 2001, the Supreme Court ruled 8 to 0 that current federal anti-drug laws provide no "medical necessity" defense against selling or growing marijuana, and that federal authorities had the discretion to obtain court orders to close down the marijuana cooperatives.[105] The Court's ruling did not, however, invalidate the medical marijuana initiatives adopted by various states in the past few years.

---

[101] 190 F. 3d, at 1114.

[102] *U.S. v. Oakland Cannabis Buyers' Cooperative*, No. C 98-0088 CRB (N.D. Cal. July 17, 2000).

[103] Sanchez, Rene. High Court Bars Calif. Clinic's Marijuana Distribution. *The Washington Post*, August 30, 2000. p. A6.

[104] *U.S. v. Oakland Cannabis Buyers' Cooperative*, 121 S. Ct 563; 2000 U.S. LEXIS 7699; 69 U.S. LW. 3363 (Nov. 27, 2000). 532 U.S.___(2001); No. 00-151, slip op. At 5 (May 14, 2001).

[105] Lane, Charles. Court Rules Against 'Medical Marijuana.' Justices Say Law Offers No Exception For Illness. *The Washington Post*, May 15, 2001. p. Al.

MEDICAL MARIJUANA AND CONGRESS: RECENT LEGISLATION

The adoption of the medical marijuana initiatives in California and Arizona in 1996 attracted a great deal of national attention and all but ensured that Congress would look for ways to get involved. In fact, the first bills introduced in the 105th Congress to deal with the medical marijuana issue - the "Medical Marijuana Deterrence Act of 1997" (H.R. 1265), and the "Medical Marijuana Prevention Act" (H.R. 1310) - were offered in response to those very state referendums. The first measure would have denied federal benefits to individuals convicted of a state offense in a state that permits medicinal use of marijuana, while the second would have given the Attorney General authority to revoke a physician's right to prescribe controlled substances if they recommend smoking marijuana for therapeutic purposes. Congress took no action on either bill.

Proposals were also introduced to assert more control over the medical marijuana issue at the federal level. One bill (H.R. 3184), would have clarified that federal controlled substances laws still apply, even in situations where state law has authorized the use and distribution of marijuana for medical purposes. Another proposal (H.R. 1469), which was also offered as an amendment to a supplemental appropriations bill, would have prohibited federal dollars from being spent to study marijuana's potential therapeutic benefits. No action was taken on the first bill; the second was withdrawn by unanimous consent.

Legislation supporting the medical use of marijuana was also proposed during the 105th Congress. Introduced by Representative Barney Frank, the "Medical Use of Marijuana Act" (H.R. 1782), would have given marijuana de facto medical recognition by legislatively transferring the drug from Schedule Ito Schedule II of the Controlled Substances Act (CSA). Moreover, the proposal would have amended both the CSA and FD&C Act so that neither statute would prohibit or restrict prescribing marijuana; prevent patients from using the drug in conjunction with a physician's orders; or prevent a licensed pharmacy from obtaining or holding marijuana for purposes of filling prescriptions. In addition, the legislation would have amended both laws so that neither could prohibit a state-established entity from producing and distributing marijuana for medical purposes. Also, the bill would have required the National Institute of Drug Abuse to make marijuana available for approved clinical investigations. No action was taken on this measure either.

Before it adjourned, however, the 105th Congress did pass a resolution expressing its support for using the traditional drug approval process for determining whether any drug, including marijuana, is safe and effective. Moreover, the legislation said that Congress opposed any effort to circumvent this process by legalizing marijuana, or any other Schedule I drug, for medical use without valid scientific evidence and the approval of the FDA. With adjournment looming, this language was incorporated into the FY 1999 omnibus appropriations act.[106] In a separate amendment in the same bill, Congress told the District of Columbia that it could not spend appropriation money to administer its own medical marijuana ballot initiative.

During the 106th Congress, Representative Frank reintroduced the "Medical Use of Marijuana Act" (HR. 912). Like its predecessor in the previous Congress, the legislation would have transferred marijuana from Schedule I to Schedule II of the Controlled Substances Act. It also would have amended the CSA and the FD&C Act so that neither law could prohibit or restrict the prescribing of marijuana; prevent patients from using it upon a doctor's order; or prevent pharmacies from obtaining marijuana in order to fill prescriptions in states where physicians can prescribe or recommend the drug for medicinal purposes. As in the previous bill, neither the CSA or the FD&C Act could prohibit or restrict a state entity from producing and distributing marijuana for medical use. Like the previous bill, it also directed the National Institute of Drug Abuse to make marijuana available for clinical trials. Finally, the act would not have affected any federal, state, or local law regulating or prohibiting smoking in public. Congress took no action on the proposal.

In September 1999, U.S. District Judge Richard Roberts issued his decision on the "Barr Amendment" (see section on State Ballot Initiatives), allowing the D.C. Board of Elections to proceed with tallying the votes on the marijuana ballot initiative considered the previous year. When the vote tally confirmed that the initiative had passed, some Members of Congress were already looking for legislative ways to keep the referendum from being implemented.

Using the appropriations process once again, Congress passed an amendment, also sponsored by Representative Barr, that would keep the District from legalizing marijuana for medical use. The amendment, part of the District's FY2000 funding bill, said that none of the appropriated monies could be used to "enact or carry out any law, rule, or regulation to legalize or otherwise reduce penalties associated with the possession, use, or distribution of any Schedule I substance under the Controlled Substances Act or any tetrahydrocannabinol derivative."[107] Furthermore, the amendment stated that the medical marijuana

---

[106] P.L. 105-277. Omnibus Consolidated and Emergency Supplemental Appropriations Act, 1999.
[107] P.L. 106-113, Section 167: Consolidated Appropriation Act, FY2000.

ballot initiative approved by D.C. voters on November 3, 1998, could not take effect. Congress imposed these same restrictions when it enacted appropriations bills for the District of Columbia for both FY2001[108] and FY2002.[109]

Thus far, two bills have been introduced in the 107th Congress (H.R. 1344 and H.R. 2592) to address the medical marijuana issue. Both pieces of legislation are sponsored by Representative Barney Frank, and both are entitled the "States' Rights to Medical Marijuana Act." Similar to the proposals introduced in the previous Congress, both bills would transfer marijuana from Schedule I to Schedule II, and at the same time amend the CSA and the FD&C Act so that neither law could prevent marijuana from being prescribed or patients from using the drugs if they have a doctor's prescription. Like before, both bills would also make it possible for pharmacies to obtain marijuana in order to fill prescriptions in those states where the drug can be prescribed. The proposals were given a title the sponsor felt would be more in concert with the various medical marijuana initiatives and laws being adopted in the states.

Although the two bills are very similar, H.R. 1344 includes a provision that would direct the National Institute on Drug Abuse (NIDA) to supply government-grown marijuana for all FDA approved clinical trials. However, when H.R. 2592 was introduced, the NIDA provision was dropped from the bill for several reasons, according to the sponsor. First of all, the sponsor thought that dropping the NIDA provision might engender broader support for the bill in Congress. It was also believed that this move would help reemphasize the main purpose of the legislation, reinforcing the right of states to determine whether doctors can prescribe marijuana. And lastly, under current federal government policy, only marijuana grown by the University of Mississippi, and supplied through NIDA, can be used in clinical trials involving smoked marijuana. Apparently, some researchers have questioned the quality of the research-grade marijuana cigarettes produced by NIDA. With this concern in mind, the sponsor felt that by introducing a second version of the bill, one without the NIDA provision, it might make it somewhat easier for researchers to do clinical studies some day without necessarily having to use marijuana supplied by the federal government.

---

[108] P.L. 106-553, Appendix A, Section 143: Appropriations for the District of Columbia, FY2001.
[109] P.L. 107-96, Section 127.

CONCLUSION

Public concern over treating AIDS and other life-threatening diseases has rejuvenated debate over whether experimental or unconventional forms of medical therapy should be made more easily available for patients suffering from such severely debilitating conditions. Encouraged by recent congressional action and subsequent changes in regulatory policies, patients are demanding earlier access to experimental therapies, including those still under clinical investigation. In the minds of medical marijuana advocates, allowing patients to smoke marijuana for medicinal purposes is nothing less than a pragmatic extension of this philosophy. Depending on the symptoms being treated, anecdotal claims by patients reinforce their view that smoking marijuana can offer modest therapeutic relief for some medical conditions. Undoubtedly, they will continue to press their belief that sufficient empirical and scientific evidence of marijuana's therapeutic utility exists to persuade government officials to reassess their traditional arguments against the drug's medical use. Without such a reassessment, especially on the national level, efforts to change state laws will surely continue.

Others, especially those who strongly support the nation's current laws criminalizing the use of marijuana, will, for the foreseeable future, remain firm in their conviction that smoking marijuana, even in small amounts, carries inherent health risks that far exceed its therapeutic benefits. To them, most current claims for marijuana's medicinal qualities remain unsupported by well-controlled clinical investigations. Although they may concede that the safety and effectiveness of synthetic dronabinol (Marinol) have been scientifically established for treating nausea and HIV wasting syndrome, they will continue to argue that the same cannot be said for the therapeutic benefits often attributed to smoked marijuana.

Currently there is a lack of public consensus and scientific agreement over the safety and medical efficacy of smoking marijuana. The National Institutes of Health Expert Group, the Institute of Medicine, and other authors have stated that there is little clinical evidence at present to support many of the medicinal claims made for smoking marijuana. They point out that existing evidence is, for the most part, anecdotal, and not strongly supported by conventional methods of scientific testing. These groups also note that smoking marijuana does not appear to offer significant therapeutic advantages over currently available prescription medications, and could impose additional health risks for some patients. Both the Expert Group and IOM, however, note that uncertainties remain, and assert that further scientific research is needed to resolve the continuing debate.

Some patients appear willing to accept these risks, and are likely to continue to push for the medicinal legitimacy of smoked marijuana. At the present time, however, there is little evidence that Congress is ready to support their objective. Instead, sentiments appear to be to the contrary. In a sense of the Congress resolution, adopted as part of an appropriations bill, the 105th Congress asserted its opinion that Schedule I drugs [e.g., marijuana] lack any currently accepted medical use, and are unsafe, even under a doctor's supervision. In the same measure, Congress stated that marijuana and other Schedule I drugs have not been approved by the FDA. Furthermore, the resolution expressed continued support of the existing federal legal process for determining the safety and efficacy of drugs, and opposed efforts to circumvent this process by legalizing marijuana, and other Schedule I drugs, for medicinal use without scientific evidence and FDA's formal approval.

Chapter 4

MARIJUANA: EARLY EXPERIENCES WITH FOUR STATES' LAWS THAT ALLOW USE FOR MEDICAL PURPOSES[*]

Paul Jones

A number of states have adopted laws that allow medical use of marijuana. Federal law, however, does not recognize any accepted medical use for marijuana and individuals remain subject to federal prosecution for marijuana possession. Debate continues over the medical effectiveness of marijuana, and over government policies surrounding medical use. A bill introduced in the House of Representatives in July 2001 would modify the federal classification of marijuana and allow doctors, in states with medical marijuana laws, to recommend or prescribe marijuana.[1] As the debate continues, so has interest in how state medical marijuana programs are operating, and in the issues faced by federal and state law enforcement officials in enforcing criminal marijuana provisions.[2]

This chapter examines the implementation of medical marijuana laws in selected states. The author did not examine the effectiveness of states' or local jurisdictions efforts to administer their programs and did not judge the validity of

---

[*] Excerpted from the United States General Accounting Office website: www.gao.gov

[1] States' Rights to Medical Marijuana Act, H.R. 2592, 107th Cong. (2001). Status as of August 5, 2002: Referred to House Energy and Commerce, Subcommittee on Health on July 31, 2001.

[2] Throughout this report, we use the phrase medical marijuana to describe marijuana use that qualifies for a medical use exception under state law.

their approaches for implementing states' laws. Oregon, Alaska, Hawaii, and California were selected because they had medical marijuana laws in effect for at least 6 months and, according to preliminary work, some data was available on patient and physician participation.[3] For these states, the author is reporting on (1) their approach to implementing their medical marijuana laws and how these approaches compare, and the results of any state audits or reviews; (2) the number, age, gender, and medical conditions of patients that have had doctors recommend marijuana for medical use in each state; (3) how many doctors are known to have recommended marijuana in each state, and what guidance is available for making these recommendations; and (4) the perceptions of federal and state law enforcement officials, and whether data are available to show how the enforcement of state marijuana laws has been affected by the introduction of these states' medical marijuana laws.

In conducting the work, applicable federal and state laws and regulations we examined and responsible program officials in Oregon, Alaska, Hawaii, and California were spoken with. In the four states, available information on program implementation, program audits, and program participation by patients and doctors were obtained and analyzed. Various federal, state, and local law enforcement officials were also met with —including officials with the Drug Enforcement Administration (DEA) and U.S. Attorneys offices in Washington, D.C., and the four selected states—to discuss data on arrests and prosecutions and views on the impact of the state's medical marijuana laws on their law enforcement efforts.

Results from the review of these states cannot be generalized to other states with state medical marijuana laws, nor are they generalizable across the states selected for review. Similarly, in California, the information from the local jurisdictions we reviewed cannot be generalized to all local jurisdictions in California.

---

[3] According to *United States v. Oakland Cannabis Buyers' Cooperative*, 532 U.S. 483, 502 n.4 (2001), eight states have enacted medical marijuana laws. We selected four of those states based on the length of time the laws had been in place and the availability of data. Two of the eight states, Nevada and Colorado, were not selected because their laws had not been in place for at least 6 months when our review began. Also, at the time of our review, two other states, Maine and Washington, did not have state registries to obtain information on program registrants. Alaska, Oregon, and Hawaii have state registries and had laws in place for at least 6 months. California's law was enacted in1996. California does not have a participant registry, but based on our preliminary work, some local registry information was available.

RESULTS IN BRIEF

State laws in Oregon, Alaska, Hawaii, and California allow medical use of marijuana under specified conditions. All four states require a patient to have a physician's recommendation to be eligible for medical marijuana use. Alaska, Hawaii, and Oregon have established state-run registries for patients and caregivers to document their eligibility to engage in medical marijuana use; these states require physician documentation of a person's debilitating condition to register. Laws in these three states also establish maximum allowable amounts of marijuana for medical purposes. California's law does not establish a state-run registry or establish maximum allowable amounts of marijuana. Some local California jurisdictions have developed their own guidelines and voluntary registries. Oregon has changed some verification practices and administrative procedures as a result of a review of their medical marijuana program.

Relatively few people had registered to use marijuana for medical purposes in Oregon, Hawaii, and Alaska. As of Spring 2002, about 2,450 people, or about 0.05 percent of the total population of the three states combined, had registered as medical marijuana users. Statewide figures for California are unknown. In Oregon, Alaska, and Hawaii, over 70 percent of registrants were over 40 years of age or older, and in Hawaii and Oregon, the two states where gender information is collected, about 70 percent of registrants were men. Data from Hawaii and Oregon also showed that about 75 percent and more than 80 percent respectively, of the physician recommendations were for severe pain and conditions associated with muscle spasms, such as multiple sclerosis. Statewide figures on gender and medical conditions were not available for Alaska or California.

Hawaii and Oregon were the only two states that had data on the number of physicians recommending marijuana. As of February 2002, less than one percent of the approximately 5,700 physicians in Hawaii and three percent of Oregon's physicians out of about 12,900 had recommended marijuana to their patients. Oregon also was the only state that maintained data on the number of times individual physicians recommended marijuana—as of February 2002, about 62 percent of the Oregon physicians recommending marijuana made one recommendation. Professional medical associations in all four states provided some guidance to physicians. The associations caution physicians about the legal issues facing them, or give advice on practices to follow and avoid. Most state medical board officials said they would only become involved with physicians recommending marijuana in cases where a complaint was filed against a physician for violating state medical practice standards. California's medical board provides informal guidelines on making marijuana recommendations to their patients.

Data were not readily available to measure how marijuana-related law enforcement has been affected by the introduction of medical marijuana laws. To assess the relationship between trends in marijuana-related law enforcement activities and the passage of medical marijuana laws would require a statistical analysis over time that included measures of law enforcement activities, such as arrests, as well as data on other factors that are not easily measured, such as changes in perceptions about marijuana and shifts in law enforcement priorities. Officials from over half of the 37 selected federal, state, and local law enforcement organizations we interviewed in the four states said that the introduction of medical marijuana laws had not greatly affected their law enforcement activities. These officials indicated that they had not encountered situations involving a medical marijuana defense or they had other drug priorities. However, officials with some of the organizations told us that the laws in their states had made it more difficult to prosecute marijuana cases where medical use might be claimed; there was confusion over how to handle seized marijuana; and that, in their view, the laws had softened public attitudes toward marijuana.

In commenting on a draft of this report, the Department of Justice (DOJ) said that we fully described the current status of the programs in the states reviewed. However, DOJ stated that we failed to adequately address some of the serious difficulties associated with such programs. Specifically, DOJ commented that the report did not adequately address issues related to the (1) inherent conflict between state laws permitting the use of marijuana and federal laws that do not; (2) potential for facilitating illegal trafficking; (3) impact of such laws on cooperation among federal, state, and local law enforcement; and (4) lack of data on the medicinal value of marijuana. DOJ further stated that our use of the phrase "medical marijuana" implicitly accepts a premise that is contrary to existing federal law.

We disagree. We believe the report adequately addresses the issues within the scope of our review. With respect to DOJ's first issue, our report describes how laws in the selected states and federal law treat the use of marijuana—the opening paragraph of our report specifically states that federal law does not recognize any accepted medical use of marijuana and individuals remain subject to federal prosecution for marijuana possession regardless of state medical marijuana laws. With regard to the second and third issues raised by DOJ concerning the potential for facilitating illegal trafficking and the impact on cooperation between federal, state, and local law enforcement officials, respectively, we interviewed federal, state, and local law enforcement officials about their perceptions concerning the impact of state medical marijuana laws on their activities and our report conveys the views and opinions of those officials. However, based on comments from law enforcement officials on a draft section of this report, we modified our report to discuss some of the issues law enforcement faces when dealing with medical marijuana laws and seized marijuana. Concerning the fourth issue—the lack of data on marijuana's medical value--our report discusses that a continuing debate exists over the medical value of marijuana, but an analysis of the scientific aspects of this debate was beyond the scope of our review.

Finally, we disagree with DOJ's comment that our use of the phrase medical marijuana accepts a premise contrary to federal law. The introduction to our report specifically states that, throughout the report, we use the phrase medical marijuana to describe marijuana use that qualifies for a medical use exception under state law.

BACKGROUND

The cannabis plant, commonly known as marijuana, is the most widely used illicit drug in the United States. According to recent national survey figures, over 75 percent of the 14 million illicit drug users 12 years or older are estimated to have used marijuana alone or with other drugs in the month prior to the survey.[4] Marijuana can be consumed in food or drinks, but most commonly dried portions of the leaves and flowers are smoked. Marijuana is widely used and the only major drug of abuse grown within the United States borders, according to the Drug Enforcement Administration.

Marijuana is a controlled substance under federal law and is classified in the most restrictive of categories of drugs by the federal government. The federal Controlled Substances Act of 1970 (CSA)[5] places all federally controlled substances into one of five "schedules," depending on the drug's likelihood for abuse or dependence, and whether the drug has an accepted medical use.[6] Marijuana is classified under Schedule I,[7] the classification reserved for drugs that have been found by the federal government to have a high abuse potential, a lack of accepted safety under medical supervision, and no currently accepted medical use.[8] In contrast, the other schedules are for drugs of varying addictive properties,

---

[4] U.S. Department of Health and Human Services, Substance Abuse and Mental Health Services Administration (SAMHSA), *National Household Survey on Drug Abuse 2000*. Hashish is included by SAMHSA in the statistic for marijuana use.

[5] 21 U.S.C. §§ 801 to 971.

[6] *Id.* § 812(a), (b).

[7] *Id.* § 812(c), Schedule I (c)(10).

[8] Schedule I includes drugs such as heroin, lysergic acid diethylamide (LSD) and other hallucinogenic substances. 21 C.F.R. 1308.11(c), (d).

but found by the federal government to have a currently accepted medical use.[9] The CSA does not allow Schedule I drugs to be dispensed upon a prescription, unlike drugs in the other schedules.[10] In particular, the CSA provides federal sanctions for possession, manufacture, distribution or dispensing of Schedule I substances, including marijuana, except in the context of a government-approved research project.[11]

The potential medical value of marijuana has been a continuing debate. For example, beginning in 1978, the federal government allowed the first patient to use marijuana as medicine under the "Single Patient Investigational New Drug" procedure, which allows treatment for individual patients using drugs that have not been approved by the Food and Drug Administration. An additional 12 patients were approved under the procedure between 1978 and 1992. When the volume of applicants tripled, the Secretary of the Department of Health and Human Services (HHS) decided not to supply marijuana to any more patients. According to *Kuromiya v. United States*, HHS concluded that the use of the single patient Investigational New Drug procedure would not yield useful data to resolve the remaining safety and effectiveness issues.[12]

In 1999, an Institute of Medicine study[13] commissioned by the White House Office of National Drug Control Policy recognized both a potential therapeutic value and potential harmful effects, particularly the harmful effects from smoked marijuana. The study called for more research on the physiological and psychological effects of marijuana and on better delivery systems. A 2001 report by the American Medical Association's Council on Scientific Affairs also summarized the medical and scientific research in this area, similarly calling for more research.[14]

---

[9] *Id.* § 812(b)(2)-(5).

[10] *Id.* § 829. DEA rejected petitions in 1992 and 2001 to reschedule marijuana to schedule II. See Notice of Denial of Petition, 66 Fed. Reg. 20038 (2001); Marijuana Scheduling Petition; Denial of Petition; Remand, 57 Fed. Reg. 10499 (1992) (final order affirming the 1989 denial after remand); Marijuana Scheduling Petition; Denial of Petition, 54 Fed. Reg. 53767 (1989).

[11] *Id.* § 823(f), 841(a)(1), 844.

[12] *See* 78 F. Supp. 2d 367 (E.D.Pa.1999). In the *Kuromiya* case, a group of approximately 160 plaintiffs raised an equal protection challenge to the administration of the "Single Patient Investigational New Drug" program. The plaintiffs contended that they were similarly situated to patients currently receiving marijuana under the program and that the government acted unconstitutionally in denying them access to the same program. The court concluded that the government had a rational basis for its decision not to supply marijuana to the plaintiffs through this program and granted the government's motion for summary judgment.

[13] National Academy of Sciences, Institute of Medicine, "Marijuana and Medicine: Assessing the Science Base." 1999.

[14] American Medical Association, Council on Scientific Affairs Report: *Medical Marijuana (A-01)*, June, 2001.

In May 1999, HHS released procedures allowing researchers not funded by the National Institute of Health to obtain research-grade marijuana for approved clinical studies. Sixteen proposals have been submitted for research under these procedures, and seven of the proposals had been approved as of May 2002.

Some states have passed laws that create a medical use exception to otherwise applicable state marijuana sanctions. California was the first state to pass such a law in 1996 when California voters passed a ballot initiative, Proposition 215 (The Compassionate Use Act of 1996) that removed certain state criminal penalties for the medical use of marijuana.[15] Since then, voters in Oregon, Alaska, Colorado, Maine, Washington and Nevada have passed medical marijuana initiatives, and Hawaii has enacted a medical marijuana measure through its legislature. While state criminal penalties do not apply to medical marijuana users defined by the state's statute, federal penalties remain, as determined by the Supreme Court in *United States v. Oakland Cannabis Buyers' Cooperative.*[16] (Appendix I provides more information on the Supreme Court's decision.)

In California, Alaska, and Oregon, where voters passed medical marijuana laws through ballot initiatives, each state provided an official ballot pamphlet, which included the text of the proposed law and arguments from proponents and opponents. Opponents of the initiatives referred to federal marijuana prohibitions, legal marijuana alternatives, and evidence of the dangers of smoked marijuana. Proponents referred to supportive studies and positive statements from medical personnel. In Hawaii, where the state legislature enacted the medical marijuana measure, law enforcement officials, advocacy groups, and medical professionals made similar arguments for or against the proposed law during the legislative process.

IMPLEMENTATION IN OREGON, ALASKA, HAWAII, AND CALIFORNIA

Oregon, Alaska, Hawaii, and California laws allow medical use of marijuana under certain conditions. [17] All four states require a patient to have a physician's

---

[15] The medical use exception in the states we reviewed allows growing or possessing marijuana for the purpose of the patient's personal medical use, and does not extend to other state marijuana prohibitions such as distribution outside the patient-caregiver relationship or any sale of marijuana.

[16] 532 U.S. 483 (2001).

[17] The states' medical marijuana laws appear at Alaska Stat. Ann. 11.71.090, 17.37.010 to 17.37.080; Cal. Health & Safety Code Ann. 11362.5; Haw. Rev. Stat. 329-121 to 329-128; and Ore. Rev. Stat. 475.300 to 475.346. Alaska's Hawaii's and Oregon's administrative regulations appear at

recommendation to be eligible for medical marijuana. Consistent with their laws, Oregon, Alaska, and Hawaii also have designated a state agency to administer patient registries—which document a patient's eligibility to use medical marijuana based on the written certification of a licensed physician—and issue cards to identify certified registrants. Also, laws in Oregon, Alaska, and Hawaii establish limits on the amounts of marijuana a patient is allowed to possess for medical purposes. California does not provide for state implementation of its law. In particular, California has not delegated authority to a state agency or established a statewide patient registry. In addition, California law does not prescribe a specific amount of marijuana that can be possessed for medical purposes. In the absence of specific statutory language, some local California jurisdictions have established their own registries, physician certification requirements, and guidelines for allowable marijuana amounts for medical purposes. Only Oregon has reviewed its medical marijuana program, and as a result of that review, has changed some of its procedures and practices, including verifying all doctor recommendations.

States and Some Local California Jurisdictions Maintain Medical Marijuana Registries

To document their eligibility to engage in medical marijuana use, applicants in Oregon, Alaska, and Hawaii must register with state agencies charged with implementing provisions of the medical marijuana laws in those states (hereinafter referred to as registry states). In Oregon, the Department of Human Services is responsible, and in Alaska, the Department of Health and Social Services. In Hawaii, the Narcotics Enforcement Division within the Department of Public Safety is responsible for the state's medical marijuana registry. Applicants meeting state requirements are entered into a registry maintained by each state. In California, a number of counties have established voluntary registries to certify eligibility under the state' s medical marijuana law.[18]

Alaska Admin. Code, tit. 7, ch. 34; Haw. Admin. R., tit. 23, ch. 202; and Ore. Admin. R., ch. 333, div. 8. There are no regulations under California's law.

[18] Under Alaska's and Hawaii's statutes, patients and caregivers must strictly comply with the registration requirement in order to receive legal protection; unregistered persons may not present a medical use defense to a marijuana prosecution in these states. *See* Alaska Stat. Ann. 11.71.090; Haw. Rev. Stat. 329-125. Under Oregon's statute, unregistered patients who have substantially complied with the act may raise such a defense to a marijuana prosecution, while registered persons are excepted from criminal charges, so long as they meet the act's quantity and use restrictions. *See* Ore. Rev. Stat. 475.306, 475.316, 475.319, 475.342. Because California's law does not establish a state-run registry, a medical use defense may be established

The three registry states, Oregon, Alaska and Hawaii, have similar registry requirements. Potential registrants must supply written documentation by a physician licensed in that state certifying that the person suffers from a debilitating medical condition (as defined by the state statute) and in the physician's opinion would benefit from the use of marijuana. They also must provide information on the name, address, and birth date of the applicant (and of their caregiver, where one is specified) along with identification to verify the personal information. In each state, registry agencies must verify the information in the application based on procedures set in that state's statutes or regulations before issuing the applicant a medical marijuana identification card. All three states allow law enforcement officers to rely upon registry applications in lieu of registry cards to determine whether a medical use exception applies. Figure 1 provides an example of the registry card issued by Oregon. (Appendix II provides examples of registry cards from Alaska and Hawaii.)

Figure 1: Example of Oregon's Medical Marijuana Registry Card

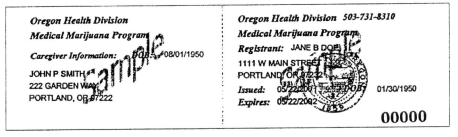

Source: Oregon Department of Human Services.

Hawaii's Department of Public Safety requires that doctors submit the completed registry application to the state agency, and if approved, the medical use certification is returned to the doctor for issuance to their patient. By contrast, registry agencies in Oregon and Alaska require that the registry card applicant submit the physician statement as part of the application, and issue the card directly to the patient. Alaska allows registry cards to be revoked if the registrant commits an offense involving a controlled substance of any type, whereas Oregon and Hawaii allow registry cards to be revoked only for marijuana-related offenses,

---

by any individual meeting the act's substantive requirements, that is, patients whose doctors have recommended marijuana to treat an allowed medical condition and their primary caregivers. *See* Cal. Health & Safety Code Ann. 11362.5; *see also People v. Mower*, No. S094490, 2002 Cal. Lexis 4520 (July 18, 2002), in which the California Supreme Court interprets California's medical marijuana act.

such as sale. Table 1 summarizes registry requirements and verification procedures of the responsible agencies in each registry state as of July 2002.

Table 1: Registry Requirements and Verification Procedures in Oregon, Alaska and Hawaii, as of July 2002

Registry requirements	Oregon	Alaska	Hawaii
Completed application form	x [a] (submitted by applicant)	x (submitted by applicant)	x (submitted by physician)
Written physician documentation	x [b]	x [c]	x [d]
Applicant name, address and date of birth. Must include a copy of a current photographic identification card, such as license, or ID card number	x	x	x
Primary caregiver name, address and date of birth. Must include a copy of a current photographic identification card, such as license, or ID card number	x	x	x
Sworn caregiver statement on department form regarding lack of felony drug conviction, not on probation or parole, and over 21		x	
Address of site where marijuana will be produced	x		x
Annual renewal for registry card	x	x	x
Minors: parents declaration form and agreement to serve as minor's caregiver	x (must be notarized)	x	x
Registration fee	$150	$25 first time $20 renewal	$25
Registry Verification Procedures			
Doctor has a valid license in state	x	x	x
Verification call or letter sent to doctor re: recommendation	x	x [e]	x
Patient contacted to validate application information	x	x [e]	x
Caregiver contacted to validate application information	x [e]	x [e]	x [e]
Registry checked to assure caregiver only serves one patient		x	

[a] A legible written statement with all the form information included will be accepted.

[b] Attending physician completes a state declaration form that the person has been diagnosed with a debilitating medical condition and that the medical use of marijuana may mitigate the symptoms or effects of the patient's condition, or applicant provides medical records of debilitating condition signed by physician that contains all information required on physician form.

[c] Signed physician statement that the patient was examined within bona fide relationship and is diagnosed with a debilitating medical condition, other medications were considered and that patient might benefit from marijuana.

[d] Signed statement that in the physician's opinion, the qualifying patient has a debilitating medical condition and the potential benefits of the medical use of marijuana would likely outweigh the health risks for the qualifying patient, OR medical records with same information.

[e] Agency officials verify when they believe it is appropriate.

Source: Oregon, Alaska, and Hawaii medical marijuana state statutes, administrative rules and program officials.

California's statute does not establish a state registry or require that a person or caregiver be registered to qualify for a medical use exception. California's law requires that medical use has been recommended by a physician who has determined that the person's health would benefit from the use of marijuana for certain symptoms or conditions. The exception applies based "upon the written or oral recommendation or approval of a physician." After the medical marijuana law was passed, the California Attorney General assembled a task force to discuss implementation issues in light of the "ambiguities and significant omissions in the language of the initiative." The task force recommended a statewide registry be created and administered by the Department of Health Services, among other things, to clarify California's law.[19] However, a bill incorporating many of the ideas agreed upon by the task force was not enacted by the California legislature.[20]

Some California communities have created voluntary local registries to provide medical marijuana users with registry cards to document that the cardholder has met certain medical use requirements. Figure 2 provides examples of patient and caregiver registry cards issued by San Francisco's Department of Public Health. (See the following section for a discussion of caregivers.)

According to a September 2000 letter by the California Attorney General, medical marijuana policies have been created in some counties. Local registries have been created in Humboldt, Mendocino, San Francisco, and Sonoma counties. A medical marijuana registry in the city of Arcata, located in Humboldt County, was discontinued, however, the Arcata police department accepts registry cards from Humboldt County. A more recent list of medical marijuana registries operated by a county or city was not available, an official with the Attorney General's office said, because there is no requirement for counties or cities to report on provisions they adopt regarding medical use of marijuana. At least two counties have since approved development of county medical marijuana registries, in San Diego in November 2001, and in Del Norte, in April 2002. Several cannabis buyers' clubs, or cannabis cooperatives may have also established voluntary registries of their members.

---

[19] Office of the Attorney General, State of California, Department of Justice, *Medical Marijuana Task Force* (July 12, 1999). Other recommendations included requiring that the patient's personal physician make the marijuana recommendation, and allowing cooperative marijuana cultivation.

[20] California Senate Bill 187, 2001-2002 Reg. Sess. The bill was introduced by California Senator Vasconcellos on February 7, 2001.

Figure 2: Example of San Francisco's Medical Marijuana Registry Cards

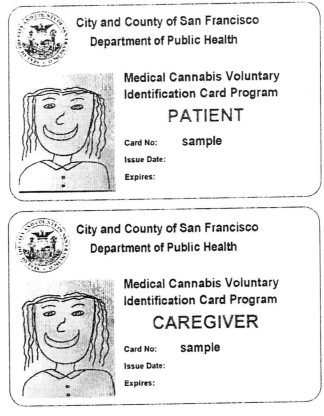

Source: San Francisco Department of Public Health.

Medical Marijuana Patient Primary Caregivers

Laws in Oregon, Alaska, Hawaii, and California allow medical marijuana users to designate a primary caregiver. To qualify as a caregiver in the registry states, persons must be part of the state registry and be issued medical marijuana cards. Registered caregivers may assist registrants in their medical use of marijuana without violating state criminal laws for possession or cultivation of marijuana, within the allowed medical use amounts. Alaska allows registrants to designate a primary and alternate caregiver. Both must submit a sworn statement that they are at least 21 years old, have not been convicted of a felony drug offense, and are not currently on probation or parole. In Hawaii and Alaska, caregivers can serve only one patient at a time. Alaska, however, allows exceptions for patients related to the caregiver by blood or marriage, or with agency approval, such as circumstances where a patient resides in a licensed hospice program. Oregon does not specify a limit to the number of patients one caregiver may serve. Table 2 provides information on definitions and caregiver provisions in Oregon, Alaska, and Hawaii.

Table 2: Definition and Provisions Regarding Caregivers in Oregon, Alaska and Hawaii

	Oregon	Alaska	Hawaii
Definition of Caregiver	"Designated primary caregiver" means an individual eighteen years of age or older who has significant responsibility for managing the wellbeing of a person who has been diagnosed with a debilitating medical condition and who is designated as such on that person's application for a registry identification card or in other written notification to the division. Designated primary caregiver does not include the person's attending physician.	"Primary caregiver" means a person listed as a primary caregiver (in the state medical use registry) and in physical possession of a caregiver registry identification card: "primary caregiver" also includes an alternate caregiver when the alternate caregiver is in physical possession of the caregiver registry identification card. "Alternate caregiver" means a person who is listed as an alternate caregiver (in the state medical use registry).	"Primary caregiver" means a person, other than the qualifying patient and the qualifying patient's physician, who is eighteen years of age or older, and who has agreed to undertake responsibility for managing the well-being of the qualifying patient with respect to the medical use of marijuana.
Limit to number of caregivers per patient	1	2 (a primary and an alternate)	1
Limit to number of patients per caregiver	Not specified	1 (exceptions may be granted by state agency)	1
Criminal record restriction on serving as caregiver	Not specified	Yes	Not specified

Source: Oregon, Alaska, and Hawaii medical marijuana statutes and administrative rules.

California's statute also allows qualified medical marijuana users to designate a primary caregiver. The statue defines "primary caregiver" to mean "the individual designated by the person exempted under this section who has consistently assumed responsibility for the housing, health or safety of that person." There is no requirement that the patient–caregiver relationship be registered or otherwise documented, nor is there a specified limit to the number of patients that can designate a particular caregiver.

Physician Recommendation Requirements

In all four states, patients must obtain a physician's diagnosis that he or she suffers from a medical condition eligible for marijuana use under that state's statute, and a physician recommendation for the use of marijuana. California does not have a requirement that the diagnosis or recommendation be documented, as the other states do. In the registry states, patients must supply written documentation of their physician's medical determination and marijuana recommendation in their registry applications. This documentation must conform with program requirements, reflecting that the physician made his or her recommendation in the context of a bona fide physician-patient relationship.

California's law does not require patients to submit documentation of a physician's determination or recommendation to any state entity, nor does it specify particular examination requirements. According to California's law, marijuana may be used for medical purposes "where that medical use is deemed appropriate and has been recommended by a physician who has determined that the person's health would benefit from the use of marijuana" in treating certain medical conditions; such recommendations may be oral or written.

The physician certification form adopted by Hawaii's Department of Public Safety calls for doctors recommending marijuana to a patient to certify that "I have primary responsibility for the care and treatment of the named patient and based on my professional opinion and having completed a medical examination and/or full assessment of my patient's medical history and current medical condition in the course of a bona fide physician-patient relationship have issued this written certificate." Similarly in Alaska, the recommending physician signs a statement that they personally examined the patient on a specific date, and that the examination took place in the context of a bona fide physician-patient relationship.

Under Oregon's medical marijuana law, the patient's attending physician must supply physician documentation. Oregon's administrative rules defining "attending physician" were amended in March 2002 to more fully describe the conditions for meeting the definition. To qualify, the physician must have established a physician-patient relationship with the patient and must diagnose the patient with a debilitating condition in the context of that relationship.[21] Agency officials stated that they changed the definition of an attending physician in light of information that one doctor responsible for many medical marijuana recommendations had not followed standard physician-patient practices, such as keeping written patient records. (See physician section.) Under its regulations, the Department of Human Services will contact each physician making a medical marijuana recommendation to assure that the physician is an "attending physician" and, with patient approval, the department may review the physician's patient file in connection with this inquiry.

Qualifying State Conditions for Use of Medical Marijuana

The laws in all four states we reviewed identify medical conditions[22] for which marijuana may be used for medical purposes. Table 3 displays the allowed medical conditions for which marijuana may be used in each state.

Allowable Amounts of Marijuana for Medical Use

Statutes in Oregon, Alaska, and Hawaii define the maximum amount of marijuana and the number of plants that an individual registrant and their caregiver may possess under medical marijuana laws, while California's statute does not provide such definitions. Oregon and Hawaii regulations also provide definitions of marijuana plant maturity. Table 4 provides the definitions of quantity and maturity for each registry state.

---

[21] As provided in Ore. Admin. R. 333-008-0010, an attending physician is "a physician who has established a physician/patient relationship with the patient, is licensed under ORS chapter 677, and who, with respect to a patient diagnosed with a debilitating medical condition: (a) Is primarily responsible for the care and treatment of the patient; (b) Is primarily responsible for recognized, medical specialty care and treatment of the patient; (c) Has been asked to consult and treat the patient by the patient's primary care physician; or (d) Has reviewed a patient's medical records at the patient's request, has conducted a thorough physical examination of the patient, has provided a treatment plan and/or followup care, and has documented these activities in a patient file."

[22] For simplicity, we use the general term medical "condition" to encompass, diseases, symptoms, and medical conditions.

Table 3: Allowable Conditions for Medical Marijuana Use in Four States

Conditions[a]	Oregon	Alaska	Hawaii	California
Cancer	x	x	x	x
Glaucoma	x	x	x	x
HIV positive status	x	x	x	
AIDS	x	x	x	x
Cachexia	x	x	x	
Wasting syndrome			x	
Anorexia				x
Epilepsy and other seizure disorders	x	x	x	
Multiple sclerosis and other disorders characterized by persistent muscle spasticity	x	x	x	x
Crohn's disease			x	
Alzheimer's disease	x			
Arthritis				x
Migraine				x
Severe pain	x	x	x	
Chronic pain				x
Severe nausea	x	x	x	
Any other illness for which marijuana provides reliefb				x

[a]Oregon's, Alaska's, and Hawaii's medical marijuana statutes use the term "debilitating medical condition" to encompass the conditions eligible for medical marijuana use. California's statute does not use this term, but simply lists the eligible conditions.

[b]California's statute does not define "any other illness for which marijuana provides relief."

Source: California, Oregon, Alaska and Hawaii medical marijuana statutes and Oregon administrative rules.

Table 4: Permissible Amounts of Medical Marijuana and Plant Maturity in Oregon, Alaska, and Hawaii

	Oregon	Alaska	Hawaii
Allowable amount	A patient and a designated primary caregiver may not individually or collectively possess more than three mature plants, four immature marijuana plants, and one ounce of usable marijuana per each mature plant, if present at a location at which marijuana is produced, including any residence associated with that location. If not at a location where marijuana is produced, including any residence associated with that location, the allowable amount is one ounce of usable marijuana.a	A patient, primary caregiver or alternate caregiver may not possess in the aggregate more than one ounce of marijuana in usable form; and six marijuana plants, with no more than three mature and flowering plants producing usable marijuana at any one time.	"Adequate Supply" means an amount of marijuana jointly possessed between the qualifying patient and the primary caregiver that is not more than is reasonably necessary to assure the uninterrupted availability of marijuana for the express purpose of alleviating the symptoms or effects of a qualifying patient's debilitating medical condition; provided that the "adequate supply" jointly possessed by the qualifying patient and the primary caregiver not exceed three mature marijuana plants, four immature marijuana plants, and one ounce of usable marijuana per each mature plant.
Plant maturity	"Mature plant" means the following: A marijuana plant shall be considered mature when male or female flower buds are readily observed on the plant by unaided visual examination. Until this sexual differentiation has taken place, a marijuana plant will be considered immature.	Not specified	"Immature marijuana plant" means a marijuana plant, whether male or female, that has not yet flowered and which does not yet have buds that are readily observed by unaided visual examination. "Mature plant" means a marijuana plant, whether male or female, that has flowered and which has buds that are readily observed by unaided visual examination.

[a]Registered patients and caregivers in Oregon who exceed the act's quantity restrictions are not immune from prosecution, but may establish an "affirmative defense" in a marijuana prosecution that the greater amount is medically necessary to mitigate the symptoms or effects of the patient's debilitating medical condition. Ore. Rev. Stat. 475.306(2).

Source: Oregon, Alaska, and Hawaii medical marijuana statutes and administrative rules.

California's statute does not specify an amount of marijuana allowable under medical use provisions; however, some local jurisdictions have established their own guidelines. The statute's criminal exemption is for "personal medical purposes" but does not define an amount appropriate for personal medical purposes. The California Attorney General's medical marijuana task force debated establishing an allowable amount but could not come to a consensus on this issue, proposing that the Department of Health Services determine an appropriate amount. Participants did agree that the amount of marijuana a patient may possess might well depend on the type and severity of illness. They concluded that an appropriate amount of marijuana was ultimately a medical issue, better analyzed and decided by medical professionals. In the absence of state specified amounts, a number of the state's 58 counties and some cities have informally established maximum allowable amounts of marijuana for medical purposes. According to the September 2000 summary by the California Attorney General's office, the amount of marijuana an individual patient and their caregiver were allowed to have varied, with a two-plant limit in one area, and a 48 plant (indoors, with mature flowers) limit in another area. In May 2002, Del Norte County raised their limit from 6 plants to 99 plants per individual patient.

Safety and Public Use Restrictions

California, Oregon, Alaska, and Hawaii prohibit medical marijuana use in specific situations relating to safety or public use. Patients or caregivers who violate these prohibitions are subject to state marijuana sanctions and, in the registry states, may also forfeit their registry cards.[23] Table 5 reflects the various states' safety or public use restrictions.

---

[23] Alaska's statute provides a one-year suspension from using or obtaining a registry card; Oregon's statute provides up to a 6-month suspension from using or obtaining a registry card; Hawaii's rules provide for revocation of the registry certificate for an indefinite time.

Table 5: Safety and Public Use Restrictions in
Oregon, Alaska, Hawaii and California

	Oregon	Alaska	Hawaii	California
Safety restrictions	Oregon's medical marijuana statute prohibits driving under the influence of marijuana.	Alaska's medical marijuana statute prohibits medical use of marijuana that endangers the health or well-being of any person.	Hawaii's medical marijuana statute prohibits medical use of marijuana that endangers the health or well-being of another person.	California's medical marijuana statute provides that, "Nothing in this section shall be construed to supersede legislation prohibiting persons from engaging in conduct that endangers others, nor to condone the diversion of marijuana for nonmedical purposes."
Public use restrictions	Oregon's medical marijuana statute prohibits patients and caregivers from engaging in the medical use of marijuana in public places as defined in Ore. Rev. Stat. 161.015, or in public view or in a correctional facility as defined in Ore. Rev. Stat. 162.135(2) or youth correction facility as defined in Ore. Rev. Stat 162.135(6).	Alaska's medical marijuana law prohibits the medical use of marijuana in plain view of, or in a place open to, the general public. The law also states that medical marijuana use need not be accommodated in any place of employment; in any correctional facility, medical facility, or facility monitored by the Alaska Department of Administration; on or within 500 feet of school grounds; at or within 500 feet of a recreation or youth center; or on a school bus.	Hawaii's medical marijuana statute prohibits the medical use of marijuana in a school bus, public bus, or any moving vehicle; in the workplace of one's employment; on any school grounds; at any public park, public beach, public recreation center, recreation or youth center; or other place open to the public.	(not specified)

[a]As defined in Ore. Rev. Stat. 161.015, a public place means a place to which the general public has access including, but not limited to, hallways, lobbies and other parts of apartment houses and hotels not constituting rooms or apartments designed for actual residence, and highways, streets, schools, places of amusement, parks, playgrounds and premises used in connection with public passenger transportation.

Source: California, Oregon, Alaska and Hawaii state statutes.

Management Review Results in Oregon Program Changes

Oregon was the only state of the four we reviewed to have conducted a management review of their state's medical marijuana program.[24] The Oregon Department of Human Services conducted the review after concerns arose that a doctor's signature for marijuana recommendations had been forged. The review team reported a number of program areas needing improvement, and proposed a corrective plan of action. Most of the actions had been completed, as of May 2002. Lack of verification of physician signature was a key problem identified by the team. All physician signatures are now verified. A number of other team findings had to do with program management and staffing. The Program Manager was replaced, additional staff was added, and their roles were clarified, according to officials. Another area of recommendation was the processing of applications and database management, such as how to handle incomplete applications, handling of voided applications, edit checks for data entry, and reducing the application backlog. As of May 2002, some action items were still open, such as computer "flags" for problem patient numbers or database checks on patients and caregivers at the same address.

FEW REGISTRANTS, MOST WITH SEVERE PAIN OR MUSCLE SPASMS

A relatively small number of people are registered as medical marijuana users in Oregon, Hawaii, and Alaska. In those states, most registrants were over 40 years old. Severe pain and muscle spasms (spasticity) were the most common medical conditions for which marijuana was recommended in the states where data was gathered.

Small Number of Medical Marijuana Registrants

Relatively few people are registered as medical marijuana users in Alaska, Hawaii and Oregon. In these states, registry data showed that the number of participants registered was below 0.05 percent or less of the total population of each respective state. Data doesn't exist to identify the total population of people with medical conditions that might qualify for marijuana use because not all the

---

[24] "Oregon's Medical Marijuana Program: A Management Review" Oregon Department of Human Services, June 11, 2001.

conditions specified in the state's laws are diseases for which population data is available. For example, a debilitating condition of "severe pain" may be a symptom for a number of specific medical conditions, such as a back injury, however not all patients with back injury suffer severe pain. Table 6 shows the number of patients registered in Oregon, Hawaii, and Alaska, at the time of our review as compared to the total population from the U.S. Census Bureau population projections for 2002.

Table 6: Medical Marijuana Registrants in Oregon, Hawaii, and Alaska, by Projected 2002 State Population

State	State population	Number of registrants	Percent of registrants by state population
Oregon	3,488,000	1,691	0.05
Hawaii	1,289,000	573	0.04
Alaska	672,000	190	0.03
Totals	**5,449,000**	**2,454**	**0.05**

Note: Oregon data as of February 2002, Alaska and Hawaii data as of April 2002.
Source: Oregon, Hawaii, and Alaska state medical marijuana registries and U.S. Bureau of the Census population projections for 2002.

There is no statewide data on participants in California because the medical marijuana law does not provide for a state registry. We obtained information from four county registries in San Francisco, Humboldt, Mendocino and Sonoma counties.[25] In each of these registries, participation was 0.5 percent or less than the respective county's population. However, because the local registries are voluntary it is unknown how many people in those jurisdictions have received medical recommendations from their doctors for marijuana but have not registered.

Table 7 shows the number of patients registered in four California counties and as a percent of the population for those counties, since each registry was established.

---

[25] Sonoma County does not maintain a "registry" of approved medical marijuana users, but is included because it does have records of county patients whose doctors have recommended marijuana using Sonoma County Medical Association peer review process.

Table 7: Registrants in Four California Counties by County Population

Registrant source	County population	Number of registrants	Percent of registrants by county population
San Francisco Department of Public Health	793,729	3551	0.44
Sonoma County Medical Association	468,754	435	0.09
Humboldt County Department of Public Health	27,754	182	0.14
Mendocino County	87,273	430	0.49

Note: San Francisco and Sonoma county data as of July 2002, Humboldt county data as of January 2002, and Mendocino county data as of April 2002.
Sources: California State Association of Counties (as of January 2002), and California medical marijuana county registries.

Medical Marijuana Registrant Demographics

Most medical marijuana registrants in Hawaii and Oregon—the states where both gender and age data were available—were males over 40 years old. Hawaii and Oregon were the only states that provided gender information; in both cases approximately 70 percent of registrants were men. In Alaska, Hawaii, and Oregon state records showed that over 70 percent of all registrants in each state were 40 years of age or older. Only in one state was there a person under the age of 18 registered as a medical marijuana user. Table 8 shows the distribution of registrants by age in the registry states.

Table 8: Registrant Age in Alaska, Hawaii and Oregon

(Percent in each age category)			
Age	**Alaska**	**Hawaii**	**Oregon**
Under 18	1 (1%)	0	0
19-29	10 (5%)	16 (3%)	145 (9%)
30-39	42 (22%)	70 (12%)	247 (15%)
40-49	84 (44%)	197 (34%)	613 (36%)
50-59	42 (22%)	216 (38%)	550 (33%)
Over 60	11 (6%)	74 (13%)	136 (8%)
Total	**190**	**573**	**1691**

Note: Oregon data as of February 2002, Alaska and Hawaii data as of April 2002.
Source: Medical Marijuana registries in Alaska, Hawaii and Oregon.

In California, none of the local jurisdictions we met with kept information on participants' gender, and only Sonoma County Medical Association provided information on their registrants' age. The age of medical association registrants was similar to participants in the state registries, only slightly younger. Over 60 percent of participants that have had their records reviewed by medical associations were 40 years or older.

Medical Marijuana Registrant Conditions

Most medical marijuana recommendations in states where data are collected have been made for applicants with severe pain or muscle spasticity as their medical condition. Conditions allowed by the states' medical marijuana laws ranged from illnesses such as cancer and AIDS, to symptoms, such as severe pain. Information is not collected on the conditions for which marijuana has been recommended in Alaska or California. However, data from Hawaii's registry showed that the majority of recommendations have been made for the condition of severe pain or the condition of muscle spasticity. Likewise, data from Oregon's registry showed that, 84 percent of recommendations were for the condition of severe pain or for muscle spasticity. Table 9 shows the number and percentage of patients registered by types of conditions in Oregon and Hawaii.

On the basis of records from the Oregon registry, we reviewed the information provided by doctors for additional insight into the conditions for which registrants use marijuana. The Oregon registry keeps track of secondary conditions in cases where the recommending doctor specified more than one condition. We examined the pool of secondary conditions associated with severe pain[26] and muscle spasms,[27] the two largest condition categories. About 40 percent of those with severe pain reported muscle spasms, migraines, arthritis, or nausea as a secondary medical condition. The most common secondary conditions reported by those with spasms were pain, multiple sclerosis, and fibromyalgia,[28] accounting for 37 percent of the secondary conditions for spasms. A variety of other secondary conditions were identified in the Oregon data, such as acid reflux,

---

[26] Of the 915 registrants that reported severe pain as their primary condition, over half reported only one secondary condition, some included up to five secondary conditions. The percentages reported here include those with only one secondary condition.

[27] Of the 459 registrants that reported spasms as a primary condition over 40 percent reported only one secondary condition, some included up to four secondary conditions. The percentages reported here include those with only one secondary condition.

[28] Fibromyalgia: Chronic pain, stiffness, and tenderness of muscles, tendons, and joints without detectable inflammation. Fatigue and sleep disorders are common in fibromyalgia patients.

asthma, chronic fatigue syndrome, hepatitis C, and lupus.

Table 9: Registrant Conditions in Oregon and Hawaii

	Oregon		Hawaii	
	Number of recommendations per condition	Percent with condition	Number of recommendations per condition	Percent with condition
Cancer	43	3	9	2
Glaucoma	31	2	10	2
HIV positive status or AIDS	47	3	66	12
Cachexia	18	1	-	-
Cachexia or wasting syndrome	-	-	9	2
Epilepsy and other seizure disorders	43	3	5	1
Multiple Sclerosis and other disorders characterized by persistent muscle spasms, or spasticity	459	28	240	43
Alzheimer's disease	1	Under 1	-	-
Severe pain	915	56	172	31
Severe nausea	83	5	12	2
Severe nausea/severe pain	-	-	31	6
Total	1640a		554b	

Note: Oregon data as of February 2002, Hawaii data as of March 2002.
[a]Information on 51 cases not available.
[b]The number of registrants for Hawaii differs in tables 8 and 9 due to differences in the reporting dates.
Source: Oregon and Hawaii medical marijuana registries.

FEW PHYSICIANS MAKE MARIJUANA RECOMMENDATIONS; SOME GUIDANCE AVAILABLE

In the two states, Hawaii and Oregon, where data on physicians is maintained, few physicians have made medical marijuana recommendations. Of the pool of recommending physicians in Oregon, most physicians made only one to two recommendations. Over half of the medical organizations we contacted provide written guidance for physicians considering recommending marijuana.

Low Physician Participation

Only a small percentage of physicians in Hawaii and Oregon were identified by state registries as having made recommendations for their patients to use marijuana as medicine. These two states maintain information on recommending physicians in their registry records. No information was available on physician participation in California and Alaska. In Hawaii, at the time of our review, there were 5,673 physicians licensed by the state's medical board. Of that number, 44 (0.78 percent) physicians had recommended marijuana to at least one of their patients since the legislation was passed in June 2000. In Oregon, at the time of our review, 435 (3 percent) of the 12,926 licensed physicians in the state had participated in the medical marijuana program since May 1999.

Both Hawaii and Oregon's medical marijuana registration programs are relatively new, which may account for the low level of participation by physicians in both states. Oregon's program has operated for a year longer than Hawaii's, however physician participation overall is low in both states. A Hawaii medical association official told us that he believes physicians consider a number of factors when deciding whether to recommend marijuana as medicine, such as the legal implications of recommending marijuana, lack of conclusive research results on the drug's medical efficacy, and a doctor's own philosophical stance on the use of marijuana as medicine.

The lower federal courts are divided in terms of whether doctors can make medical marijuana recommendations without facing federal enforcement action, including the revocation of doctors' DEA registrations that allow them to write prescriptions for federally controlled substances. In one case, the district court for the Northern District of California held that the federal government could not revoke doctors' registrations, stating that the de-registration policy raised "grave constitutional doubts" concerning doctors' exercise of free speech rights in making medical marijuana recommendations.[29] In the other case considering this issue, the district court for the District of Columbia ruled that the federal government could revoke doctors' registrations, stating that "[e]ven though state law may allow for the prescription or recommendation of medicinal marijuana within its borders, to do so is still a violation of federal law under the CSA," and

---

[29] *See Conant v. McCaffrey*, No. C-97-00139, 2000 U.S. Dist. LEXIS 13024 at *19 (N.D. Cal. Sept. 7, 2000) (permanent injunction granted); *see also Conant v. McCaffrey*, 172 F.R.D. 681 (N.D. Cal. 1997) (preliminary injunction granted). On October 29, 2002, the Ninth Circuit Court of Appeals affirmed, finding that the district court convincingly explained how the government's professed enforcement policy threatened to interfere with doctors' First Amendment rights. *See Conant v. Walters*, No. 00-17222, 2002 U.S. App. LEXIS 22942 at *2 (9th Cir. Oct. 29, 2002)

"there are no First Amendment protections for speech that is used 'as an integral part of conduct in violation of a valid criminal statute.'"[30]

Oregon is the only state we reviewed which has registry records that identify recommendations by doctor. Few Oregon physicians made recommendations to use medical marijuana to more than two patients. According to registry data, 82 percent of the participating physicians made one or two recommendations, and 18 percent made three or more recommendations. Table 10 shows a breakdown of the frequency by which physicians made marijuana recommendations.

Table 10: Number of Marijuana Recommendations made by Oregon Physicians, as of February 2002

Number of recommendations	Number of physicians making recommendations	Percentage of recommending physicians
1	269	61.8
2	87	20.0
3	33	7.6
4	22	5.1
5	8	1.8
6	2	0.5
7	2	0.5
9	2	0.5
10	1	0.2
11	1	0.2
12	1	0.2
13	2	0.5
14	1	0.2
18	1	0.2
23	1	0.2
38	1	0.2
823	1	0.2

Source: Oregon Department of Human Services.

State or law enforcement officials in Oregon, California, and Hawaii indicated that they were each aware of a particular physician in their state that had

---

[30] *See Pearson v. McCaffrey*, 139 F. Supp. 2d 113, 121 (D.D.C. 2001).

recommended marijuana to many patients.[31] In Alaska, a state official knew of no physician that had made many recommendations. In Oregon and California the state medical boards have had formal complaints filed against these physicians for alleged violations of the states' Medical Practices Acts, which establish physician standards for medical care. The complaints charge the physicians with unprofessional conduct violations such as failure to conduct a medical examination, failure to maintain adequate and accurate records, and failure to confer with other medical care providers. In Oregon, the physician recommending marijuana to over 800 patients was disciplined.[32] The California case was still pending. At the time of our review, there was no medical practice complaint filed against the Hawaiian doctor known to have made many marijuana recommendations.

Physician Guidance for Making
Medical Marijuana Recommendations

In all four states, professional medical associations provide some guidance for physicians in regards to recommending marijuana to patients. State medical boards, in general, have limited involvement in providing this type of guidance. Table 11 indicates the type of guidance available from these medical organizations in each state.

The guidance to physicians considering recommending marijuana to a patient in Oregon, for example, includes avoiding engaging in any discussions with a patient on how to obtain marijuana, and to avoid providing a patient with any written documentation other than that in the patient's medical records. The medical association also advises physicians to clearly document in a patient's medical records conversations that take place between the physician and patient about the use of marijuana as medicine. Oregon's medical association notes that until the federal government advises whether it considers a physician's medical marijuana recommendation in a patient chart to violate federal law, no physician is fully protected from federal enforcement action.

---

[*] Program officials in the registry states verify that a physician recommendation has been made in accordance with program requirements, and that the physician is licensed; they are not authorized to determine whether a doctor's recommendation is medically appropriate.

[*] The April 2002 order by the Oregon Board of Medical Examiners reprimanded the physician, fined him $5,000, suspended his license for 90 days, and specified conditions under which any future marijuana recommendations would be made, and other disciplinary actions.

Table 11: Doctor Guidance Provided by Selected State Medical Organizations

State Medical Organizations	Guidance provided	Description
Oregon State Board of Medical Examiners	No	
Oregon Medical Association	Yes	The association has a document informing members of the legal issues facing doctors and advising them on doctor-patient discussions and documentation concerning the use of marijuana for medicine, and actions to avoid.
Alaska State Medical Board	No	
Alaska Medical Association	Yes	Those inquiring about recommending marijuana are directed to seek legal counsel.
Hawaii State Board of Medical Examiners	No	
Hawaii Medical Association	Yes	Those inquiring about recommending marijuana are informed of the association's official position against medical marijuana and advised of the legal implications involved.
Medical State Board of California	Yes	The board has a document that describes the standards physicians recommending marijuana should apply to their practice and advises them on how to best protect themselves.
California Medical Association	Yes	The association provides a document covering the legal issues facing doctors, doctor-patient discussions and documentation concerning the use of marijuana for medicine, actions to avoid, and other topics under the law that may be of concern to physicians.

Note: Guidance provided as of the time of our review.
Source: State Medical Boards and Medical Associations in Oregon, Alaska, Hawaii, and Oregon.

Most of the state medical board officials we contacted stated that the medical boards do not provide guidance for physicians on recommending marijuana to patients. The medical boards do become involved with physicians making marijuana recommendations if a complaint for violating state medical practices is filed against them. Once a complaint is filed, the boards investigate a physician's practice. Any subsequent action occurs if the allegations against a doctor included violations of the statutes regulating physician conduct.

California medical board's informal guidance states that physicians recommending marijuana to their patients should apply the accepted standards of medical responsibility such as the physical examination of the patient, development of a treatment plan, and discussion of side effects. In addition, the board warns physicians that their best legal protection is by documenting how they arrived at their decision to recommend marijuana as well as any actions taken for the patient.

DIFFICULT TO MEASURE THE IMPACT OF STATE MEDICAL MARIJUANA LAWS ON LAW ENFORCEMENT ACTIVITIES

Data are not readily available to show whether the introduction of medical marijuana laws have affected marijuana-related law enforcement activities. Assessing such a relationship would require a statistical analysis over time that included measures of law enforcement activities, such as arrests, as well as other measures that may influence law enforcement activities. It may be difficult to identify the relevant measures because crime is a sociological phenomena influenced by a variety of factors.[33] Local law enforcement officials we spoke with about trends in marijuana law enforcement noted several factors, other than medical marijuana laws, important in assessing trends. These factors included changes in general perceptions about marijuana, shifts in funding for various law enforcement activities, shifts in local law enforcement priorities from one drug to another, or changes in emphasis from drugs to other areas, such as terrorism. Demographics might also be a factor.

The limited availability of data on marijuana-related law enforcement activity illustrates some of the difficulties in doing a statistically valid trend analysis. To fully assess the relationship between the passage of state's medical marijuana laws and law enforcement, one would need data on marijuana related arrests or prosecutions over some period of time, and preferably an extended period of time.

---

[33] According to the FBI introduction to users of Uniform Crime Report data.

Although state-by-state data on marijuana-related arrests is available from the FBI Uniform Crime Reports (UCR), at the time of our review, only data up to the year 2000 was available. Yearly data would be insufficient for analytic purposes since the passage of the medical marijuana initiatives or law in three of the states— Oregon (November 1998), Alaska (November 1998), and Hawaii (June 2000)—is too recent to permit a rigorous appraisal of trends in arrests and changes in them.[34] Furthermore, although California's law took effect during 1996 providing a longer period of data, it is also important to note that the FBI cautions about UCR data comparisons between time periods because of variations in year-to-year reporting by agencies.[35]

Similar data limitations would occur using marijuana prosecutions as a measure of trends in law enforcement activity. Data on marijuana prosecutions are not collected or aggregated at the federal level by state. At the state level, for the four states we reviewed, the format for collecting the data, or time period covered also had limitations. For example in California, the state maintains "disposition" data that includes prosecutions, but reflects only the most serious offenses, so that marijuana possession that was classified as a misdemeanor would not be captured if the defendant was also charged with possession of other drugs, or was involved with theft or other non-misdemeanor crimes. Further, the data is grouped by the year of final disposition, not when the offense occurred. Hawaii does not have statewide prosecution data. At the time of our review, prosecution data from Oregon's statewide Law Enforcement Data System was only available for 1999 and 2000.

Perceptions of Officials with Selected Law Enforcement Organizations Regarding the Impact of Medical Marijuana Laws

We interviewed officials from 37 selected federal, state, and local law enforcement organizations in the four states to obtain their views on the effect, if

---

[34] Programs to implement the laws in Oregon, Alaska and Hawaii were developed somewhat later. Alaska's registry was established in June 1999, Oregon's program began operating in May 1999, and Hawaii issued its first card in January 2001.

[35] As described in the methodology section of UCR's annual publication, *Crime in the United States* (2000) UCR excludes trend statistics if the reporting units have not provided comparable data for the periods under consideration, or when it is ascertained that unusual fluctuations, such as improved record keeping or annexations are involved. Although most law enforcement agencies submit crime reports to the UCR program, data are sometimes not received for complete annual periods. If data on other factors was available for California to analyze the relationship of its medical marijuana law and arrests, one would also need to assess the comparability of arrest data from different time periods.

any, state medical marijuana laws had on their law enforcement activities. Officials representing 21 of the organizations we contacted indicated that medical marijuana laws had had little impact on their law enforcement activities for a variety of reasons, including very few or no encounters involving medical marijuana registry cards or claims of a medical marijuana defense. For example:

- The police department on one Hawaiian island had never been presented a medical marijuana registry card, and only 15 registrants lived on the island.
- In Alaska, a top official for the State Troopers Drug Unit had never encountered a medical marijuana registry card in support of claimed medical use.
- In Oregon, one district attorney reported having less than 10 cases since the law was passed where the defendant presented a medical marijuana defense.[36]
- In Los Angeles County, an official in the District Attorney's office stated that only three medical marijuana cases have been filed in the last two years in the Central Branch office, two of the cases involving the same person.

Some of the federal law enforcement officials we interviewed indicated that the introduction of medical marijuana laws has had little impact on their operations. Senior Department of Justice officials said that the Department's overall policy is to enforce all laws regarding controlled substances, however they do have limited resources. Further, the federal process of using a case-by-case review of potential marijuana prosecutions has not changed as a consequence of the states' medical marijuana laws. These officials said that U.S. Attorneys have their own criteria or guidelines for which cases to prosecute that are based on the Department's overall strategies and objectives.

Law enforcement officials in the selected states also told us that, given the range of drug issues, other illicit drug concerns, such as rampant methamphetamine abuse or large-scale marijuana production are higher priorities than concerns about abuse of medical marijuana. In at least one instance, this emphasis was said to reflect community concerns—in Hawaii, one prosecuting attorney estimated that one-third to one-half of the murders and most hostage situations in the county involved methamphetamines. He said businesses ask why

---

[36] The District Attorney noted that they had won these cases because the defendants were not operating within the parameters of the state medical marijuana law.

law enforcement is bothering with marijuana when they have methamphetamines to deal with.

Although many of the officials with other organizations we contacted did not clearly indicate whether medical marijuana laws had, or had not, had major impact on their activities, officials with two organizations said that medical marijuana laws had become a problem from their perspective. Specifically, an official with the Oregon State Police Drug Enforcement Section said that during 2000 and 2001, there were 14 cases in which the suspects had substantial quantities of processed or growing marijuana and were arrested for distribution of marijuana for profit, yet were able to obtain medical marijuana registry cards after their arrests. Because the same two defense attorneys represented all the suspects, the police official expressed his view that the suspects might have been referred to the same doctor, causing the official to speculate about the validity of the recommendations. In Northern California—an area where substantial amounts of marijuana are grown[37]—officials with the Humboldt County Drug Task Force[38] told us that they have encountered growers claiming to be caregivers for multiple medical marijuana patients. With a limit of 10 plants per person established by the Humboldt County District Attorney, growers can have hundreds of plants officials said, and no documentation to support their medical use claims is required.[39]

Over one-third of officials from the 37 law enforcement organizations told us that they believe that the introduction of medical marijuana laws have, or could make it, more difficult to pursue or prosecute some marijuana cases. In California, some local law enforcement officials said that their state's medical marijuana law makes them question whether it is worth pursuing some criminal marijuana cases because of concerns about whether they can effectively prosecute (e.g., with no statutory limit on the number of marijuana plants allowed for medical use, the amount consistent with a patient's personal medical purposes is open to interpretation). In Oregon, Hawaii, and Alaska where specific plant limits have been established, some law enforcement officials and district attorneys said that they were less likely to pursue marijuana cases that could be argued as falling under medical use provisions. For example, one Oregon District Attorney stated that because they have limited resources the District Attorneys might not prosecute a case where someone is sick, has an amount of marijuana within the

---

[37] According to the senior DEA official for the area, three northern counties are the source region for much of the domestically produced marijuana in the United States, and this production is a major contributor to the local economies.

[38] Headed by a Commander from the California Bureau of Narcotics and staffed by officers from local law enforcement.

[39] The 10 plant limit can be exceeded if the grower claims to grow 10 plants for patient A, 10 plants for patient B, and so on. Documentation of caregiver status is not required under the state's law.

medical use limit, and would probably be approved for a card if they did apply. Officers in Hawaii reported reluctance of a judge to issue a search warrant until detectives were certain that cultivated marijuana was not being grown for medical use, or that the growth was over the 25-plant limit qualifying for felony charges.

Less concrete, but of concern to law enforcement officials were the more subtle consequences attributed to the passage of state medical marijuana laws. Officials in over one-fourth of the 37 law enforcement organizations we interviewed indicated they believe there has been a general softening in public attitude toward marijuana, or public perception that marijuana is no longer illegal. For example, state troopers in Alaska said that they believe that the law has desensitized the public to the issue of marijuana, reflected in fewer calls to report illegal marijuana activities than they once received. Hawaiian officers stated that it is their view that Hawaii's law may send the wrong message because people may believe that the drug is safe or legal.

Several law enforcement officials in California and Oregon cited the inconsistency between federal and state law as a significant problem, particularly regarding how seized marijuana is handled. According to a California Attorney General official, state and local law enforcement officials are frequently faced with this issue if the court or prosecutor concludes that marijuana seized during an arrest was legally possessed under California law, and law enforcement is ordered to return the marijuana. To return it puts officials in violation of federal law for dispensing a Schedule I narcotic, according to the California State Sheriffs' Association, and in direct violation of the court order if they don't return it. The same issue has arisen in Portland, Oregon, officials said, when the Portland police seized 2.5 grams of marijuana from an individual. After the state dismissed charges, the court ordered the return of the marijuana to the individual, who was a registered medical marijuana user. The city of Portland appealed the court order on grounds that its police officers could not return the seized marijuana without violating federal law, but the Oregon court of appeals rejected this argument in *Oregon v. Kama*.[40] Oregon officials said that DEA then obtained a federal court order

---

[40] 39 P.3d 866 (Or. Ct. App. 2002); *rev. den.* 47 P.3d 484 (Or. S. Ct. 2002). In *Kama*, the city argued that, because marijuana is a Schedule I controlled substance, its police officers would commit the federal crime of delivering a controlled substance if they returned seized marijuana. The court of appeals disagreed, reasoning that the federal Controlled Substances Act, 21 U.S.C. 885(d), confers immunity on state or local law enforcement officials "lawfully engaged in the enforcement of any law or municipal ordinance relating to controlled substances." The court concluded that, because the officers were required to return the seized marijuana under Oregon's

to seize the marijuana from the Portland police department. The Department of Justice stated in comments on a draft of this report that they believe conflicts between federal and non-federal law enforcement over the handling of seized marijuana has been and will continue to be a problem.

Law enforcement officials in all four states identified areas of their medical marijuana laws that can hamper their marijuana enforcement activities because the law could be clearer or provide better control. In California, key issues were lack of a definable amount of marijuana for medical use, and no systematic way to identify who qualifies for the exemption. In Oregon, officers were concerned about individuals registering as medical marijuana users after they have been arrested, and timely law enforcement access to the registry information. Officials with about one-fourth of the law enforcement organizations in Hawaii, California and Oregon shared the concern about the degree of latitude given to physicians in qualifying patients for medical use.

APPENDIX I: THE SUPREME COURT'S DECISION IN *UNITED STATES V. OAKLAND CANNABIS BUYERS' COOPERATIVE*

Under the federal Controlled Substances Act of 1970 (CSA), marijuana is classified as a Schedule I controlled substance, a classification reserved for drugs found by the federal government to have no currently accepted medical use. 21 U.S.C. 812(c), Schedule I (c)(10).

Consistent with this classification system, the CSA does not allow Schedule I drugs to be dispensed upon a prescription, unlike drugs in the less restrictive drug schedules. *Id.* 829. In particular, the CSA prohibits all possession, manufacture, distribution or dispensing of Schedule I substances, including marijuana, except in the context of a governmentapproved research project. *Id.* 823(f), 841(a)(1), 844.

Some states have passed laws that create a medical use exception to otherwise applicable state marijuana sanctions. California was the first state to pass such a law, when, in 1996, California voters passed a ballot initiative, Proposition 215, which removed certain state criminal penalties for the medical use of marijuana.

In the wake of Proposition 215, various cannabis clubs formed in California to provide marijuana to patients whose physicians had recommended such treatment. In 1998, the United States sued to enjoin one of these clubs, the Oakland Cannabis Buyers' Cooperative, from cultivating and distributing

---

medical marijuana act, Or. Rev. Stat. 475.323(2), federal law granted them immunity for doing so.

marijuana. The United States argued that, whether or not the Cooperative's actions were legal under California law, they violated the CSA. Following lower court proceedings, the U.S. Supreme Court granted the government's petition for a writ of certiorari to review whether the CSA permitted the distribution of marijuana to patients who could establish "medical necessity." *United States v. Oakland Cannabis Buyers' Cooperative*, 532 U.S. 483 (2001).

Although the tension between California's Proposition 215 and the broad federal prohibition on marijuana was the backdrop for the *Oakland Cannabis* case, the legal issue addressed by the Supreme Court did not involve the constitutionality of either the federal or state statute. Rather, the Court confined its analysis to an interpretation of the CSA and whether there was a medical necessity defense to the Act's marijuana prohibitions. The Court held that there was not. While observing that the CSA did not expressly abolish the defense, the Court stated that the statutory scheme left no doubt that the defense was unavailable for marijuana. Because marijuana appeared in Schedule I, it reflected a determination that marijuana had no currently accepted medical use for purposes of the CSA. The Court concluded that a medical necessity defense could not apply under the CSA to a drug determined to have no medical use.

The *Oakland Cannabis* case upheld the federal government's power to enforce federal marijuana prohibitions without regard to a claim of medical necessity. Thus, while California (and other states) exempt certain medical marijuana users and their designated caregivers from state sanctions, these individuals remain subject to federal sanctions for marijuana use.

APPENDIX II: MEDICAL MARIJUANA REGISTRIES IN OREGON, ALASKA, HAWAII, AND SELECT CALIFORNIA COUNTIES

How states implemented registry requirements in the three registry states, such as which agency administers the registry or the number of staff to manage it, varied in some ways and were similar in other ways. Similarly, the county-based registries in California had some differences and commonalities.

Oregon

In Oregon, the Department of Human Services is designated to maintain the state medical marijuana registry. A staff of six is responsible for reviewing and verifying incoming applications and renewals, including following up on those that are incomplete, and input and update of the database. Recommending physicians are sent, and must respond to a verification letter for the application to be approved. By statute in Oregon, an applicant can be denied a card for only two reasons—submitting incomplete or false information. According to the State Public Health Officer, the scope of the Department of Human Services responsibility is to see to that there is a written determination of the patient's condition by a legitimate doctor, and includes an attending physician recommendation that the patient might benefit from using marijuana. He stated that the staff does not question a doctor's recommendation for medical marijuana use. The law is clear, he said. It is up to the physician to decide what is best.

The Oregon Department of Human Services also considers the addition of new conditions to the list of those acceptable for medical use of marijuana, as authorized by Oregon's medical marijuana statute. At the time of our review, only one of the eight petitions that had been reviewed by the Department had been approved—agitation due to Alzheimer's disease. Most of the petitioned conditions have had a psychological basis, the State Public Health Officer said.

Alaska

Alaska's statute designates the Department of Health and Social Services to manage the state medical marijuana registry. The full time equivalent of one half-time person is responsible for registry duties, including checking applications for accuracy and completeness and entering the information into the registry. The physician's license is checked for approval to practice in Alaska, and if a caregiver is designated the registry is checked to assure they are only listed as a caregiver for one person unless otherwise approved by the Department. Patients, physicians and caregivers are also contacted to verify information as appropriate. If all Alaska statutory requirements are met, a medical marijuana registry identification card is issued (see fig. 4). Registry cards are denied in Alaska if the application is not complete, the patient is not otherwise qualified to be registered, or if the information in the application is found to be false.

Figure 3: Example of Alaska's Medical Marijuana Certification Card

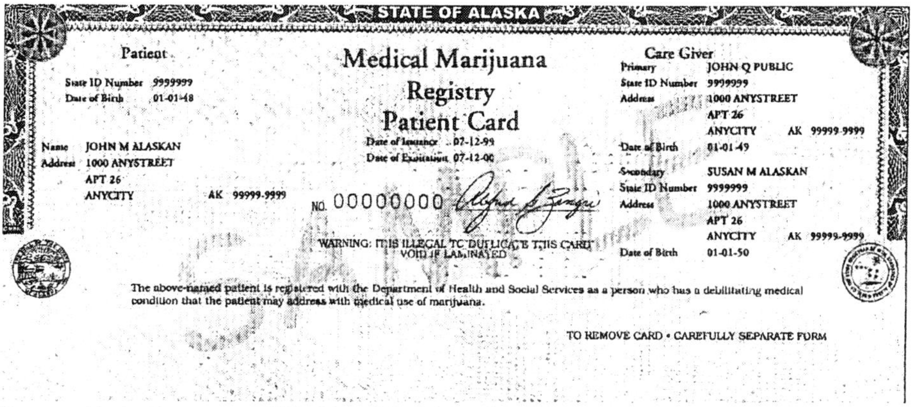

Source: Alaska Department of Health and Social Services.

Alaska's statute allows the Department to add debilitating medical conditions to the approved list for use of marijuana. A procedure for requesting new conditions is outlined in state regulations. To date, there have been no requests to consider new conditions and none have been added.

Hawaii

The medical marijuana law passed by the Hawaiian legislature designates the state Department of Public Safety to administer the Hawaiian medical marijuana registry. One person within Public Safety's Narcotics Enforcement Division staffs the registry. This person is responsible for reviewing and approving applications and renewals as complete, inputting applicant information into the database, and responding to any law enforcement inquiries. Verification procedures in Hawaii are similar to those followed in other states. See figure 4 for an example of Hawaii's registry card.

Figure 4: Example of Hawaii's Medical Marijuana Registry Card

State of Hawaii
Department of Public Safety
Narcotics Enforcement Division
Medical Marijuana Registry
Patient Identification Certificate

Patient: **ALOHA, LEI**
             789 Malihini Street

             Honolulu, HI 96816
DOB: 12/31/2000
Patient ID No.:   123-12-1234

Caregiver: PALANI KING
567 Date Street

Honolulu, HI 96870
Caregiver ID No.:   H0006789
Location of Marijuana:

Physician: JOHN A APPLEWAY, md

_____
            Physician's Signature

Expiration Date: 1/31/2003

Registration No.:   **MJ50000**

_____
            Division Administrator

WARNING: IT IS ILLEGAL TO DUPLICATE THIS CARD
LLAW 0225 (12-00)

Source: State of Hawaii Department of Public Safety.

California

Registration application requirements and procedures for the voluntary California registries we reviewed were unique to each county, but shared some procedures with the programs established in the registry states.

In Humboldt County, the patient must submit an application and physician recommendation to the county Department of Health and Human Services, with a $40.00 fee. Applicants are interviewed, photographed, and their county residency documents are checked during an in-person interview. To protect the confidentiality of doctors, after the physician recommendation has been verified, the physician portion of the application is detached and shredded. Applications are denied if the patient is not a county resident, the physician is not licensed in California, or there is not a therapeutic relationship between the patient and physician.

The San Francisco Medical Cannabis ID Card Program applications are made available through the city's Department of Public Health, where the registry is maintained, and also from clinics, doctor's offices and medical cannabis organizations that have requested them. Applicants must bring a physician's statement form, or form documenting that an oral recommendation was received, medical records release form, proof of identification and residence in San Francisco and the fee. For an applicant the fee is $25.00, plus $25.00 for each primary caregiver, up to a maximum of three caregivers. Registry cards are valid for up to 2 years, based on a physician's recommendation. After verifying the application documents to its satisfaction, the Department returns the entire application package to the applicant, and issues cards to the applicant and caregivers. The department does not copy the materials, or keep the name of registrants. Information kept on file is limited to the serial number of the cards issued, the serial number of the identification card submitted, the date the registry card was issued, and when it expires.

The Mendocino County Public Heath Department and the Sheriff's office jointly run the County Pre-identification Program for county residents. The Health Department accepts the applicant's Medical Marijuana Authorization forms, which includes patient and caregiver information, and a section for the physician to complete. The physician section requires checking "yes" or "no" to a recommendation, and the expiration length for the recommendation in months, years or for the patient's lifetime. No condition information is requested. After verifying the physician recommendation, that section is destroyed, and the approved authorization sheet is sent to the Sheriff's office. The Sheriff's office interviews registrants and caregivers, requiring that they sign a declaration as to the caregiver's role in patient care. Program identification cards with photographs of patients and caregivers are issued by the Sheriff's office.

In Sonoma County, the Sonoma County Medical Association, in conjunction with the Sonoma County District Attorney, developed a voluntary process for the medical association to provide peer review of individuals' medical records and physician recommendations for medical use of marijuana. Based on the review, the patient's physician is sent a determination regarding whether the patient's case met criteria established regarding the patient-physician relationship, whether marijuana was approved of, and whether the condition is within the California state code allowing medical marijuana use. Upon receiving the determination from their doctor, patients decide whether to voluntarily submit the results to the District Attorney for distribution to the appropriate police department or to the sheriff's office. According to the medical association director, some patients will go through the process but prefer to keep the letter themselves rather than have their name in a law enforcement database.

Chapter 5

MARIJUANA FOR MEDICAL PURPOSES: THE SUPREME COURT'S DECISION IN *UNITED STATES V. OAKLAND CANNABIS BUYERS' COOPERATIVE* AND RELATED LEGAL ISSUES

Charles Doyle

SUMMARY

In *United States* v. *Oakland Cannabis Buyers' Cooperative,* 532 U.S.483 (2001), the United States Supreme Court held, without dissent, that there is no medical necessity defense to the federal law prohibiting cultivation and distribution of marijuana - even in states which have created a medical marijuana exception to a comparable ban under state law.

Congress classified marijuana as a Schedule I controlled substance, a classification it reserved for those substances which have no currently accepted medical use in the United States. Therefore, the Court concluded, Congress could hardly have intended to recognize a medical necessity defense for marijuana and recognition of any such defense would be contrary to Congress' clear intentions.

The Coop raised three constitutional issues in its brief before the Court. It suggested that a federal medical marijuana ban would exceed the reach of Congress' authority to regulate interstate commerce; that such a ban would be contrary to the constitutional reservation of powers to the people; and that such a ban would be contrary to the substantive due process rights of patients who use marijuana for medical reasons. The Court did not address the constitutional issues suggested in the Coop's brief because the lower court decision under review did not rule upon them. Other courts have disagreed over whether enforcement of the ban against physicians is contrary to their First Amendment right to free speech.

The Court's description of matters within Congress' legislative authority under the commerce clause in *United States v. Lopez* and *United States v. Monison* indicates that the federal ban on the cultivation, distribution or possession of marijuana lies within Congress' prerogatives. Its characterization of the limitations on the enacting clause in *Prim v. United States* and of the circumstances warranting expanded substantive due process recognition in *Washington v. Glucksberg* encumber the Coop's contentions on those counts.

Related legislative activity in this Congress includes a proposal for an exception to the federal prohibitions in those states whose laws allow use of marijuana for medicinal purposes.

INTRODUCTION

There is no medical necessity defense to the federal crimes of cultivating or distributing marijuana. So said the Supreme Court in *United States v. Oakland Cannabis Buyers' Cooperative*, 532 U.S. 483,486 (2001). The Court left undecided questions over whether a necessity defense might be available for possession and over possible commerce clause, enactment clause, and due process clause challenges.

BACKGROUND

The federal Controlled Substances Act (the Act) outlaws the cultivation, distribution, or possession of marijuana, 21 U.S.C. 841, 844.[1] The ban is a

---

[1] Strictly speaking, sections 841 and 844 proscribe the unlawful manufacture, distribution, dispensing, or possession of controlled substances. Marijuana is classified as a Schedule I controlled substance, 21 U.S.C. 812(c), Sch. I(c)(10). "Manufacturing" means "production, preparation, propagation, compounding or processing," 21 U.S.C. 802(15), and "production" includes "planting, cultivation, growing, or harvesting of a controlled substance," 21 U.S.C. 802(22). Schedule I is reserved for those controlled substances which (A) have "a high potential for abuse," (B) have "no currently accepted medical use in treatment in the United States," and (C) for which "[t]here is a lack of accepted safety for use ... under medical supervision," 21 U.S.C. 812(b)(l). Consequently, physicians may not ordinarily prescribe Schedule I controlled substances, 21 U.S.C. 829 (prescriptions for Schedule II, in, IV and V controlled substances),

component of federal and state schemes which regulate the sale and possession of drugs and other controlled substances. The State of California has created a medical necessity exception to its marijuana prohibitions, CAL. HEALTH & SAFETY CODE ANN. §11362.5.[2] The Oakland Cannabis Buyers Cooperative (the Coop) was one of the entities which dispensed marijuana to patients qualified to receive it under state law.

Federal authorities sued to enjoin cultivation and distribution of marijuana in violation of federal law by the Coop and its suppliers. The federal district court granted a preliminary injunction, *United States v. Cannabis Cultivators Club, 5 F.Supp. 2d 1086 (N.D.Cal. 1998),* which the Court of Appeals overturned for failure to consider an implicit medical necessity defense, *United States v. Oakland Cannabis Buyers Cooperative,* 190F.3d 1109 (9th Cir. 1999).

The necessity or "choice of evils" defense has been recognized by a number of other lower federal appellate courts.[3] The Supreme Court seemed to verify its vitality, at least indirectly, when it described the prerequisites for the defense to an escape charge: "where a criminal defendant is charged with escape and claims that he is entitled to an instruction on the theory of duress or necessity, he must proffer evidence of a bona fide effort to surrender or return to custody as soon as the claimed ... necessity has lost its coercive force," *United States v. Bailey,* 444 U.S. 394,415 (1980).

SUPREME COURT DECISION

The Coop argued that necessity, as a common law defense, was an implicit exception to the Act's prohibitions. No member of the Supreme Court agreed, 532

---

and manufacturing and distributing Schedule I controlled substances for research purposes is tightly regulated, 21 U.S.C. 822,823. The Attorney General, acting with the benefit of the recommendations of the Secretary of Health and Human Services, is authorized to assign and reassign substances to the appropriate schedules, 21U.S.C.811. An abbreviated form of this report is available under the title, *Marijuana for Medical Purposes: A Glimpse of the Supreme Court's Decision in United States v. Oakland Cannabis Buyers' Cooperative and Related Legal Issues,* CRSREP.NO.RS20998 (April 15,2002). Penalties authorized for violations of the Act are discussed in, Doyle, *Drug Smuggling, Drug Dealing and Drug Abuse: Background and Overview of the Sanctions Under the Federal Controlled Substances Act and Related Statutes,* CRS REP. No. 97-141 (Oct.27, 2000).

[2] Several other states have "medical marijuana" laws, ALASKA STAT. §11.71.090; ARIZ. REV.STAT.ANN. §13-3412.01(A); COLO. CONST. Art. XVIII §4; HAWAII REV.STAT. §§329-121 to 329-128; ME. REV.STAT.ANN. tit.22 §1102 or 2382-B(5); NEV. REV.STAT.ANN. §§453A010 to 453A400; ORE.REV.STAT. §§475.300 to 475.346; WASH. REV.CODE ANN. §§69.51A005 to 69.51A902.

U.S. at 490.[4] In feet, a majority questioned the very existence of a federal necessity defense,[5] although as the concurring opinion points out, the case holds no more than that there is no necessity defense to the federal proscription on the cultivation or distribution of marijuana.[6]

On the basic point, the members of the Court were of one mind - Congress in the Act addressed and rejected the very exception for which the Coop sought recognition. Congress outlawed manufacturing or distributing controlled substances except as authorized in the Act, 21 U.S.C. 841(a)(l). The only authorized exception for Schedule I controlled substances, such as marijuana, is government approved research, 21U. S .C. 823(f); the Coop did not argue that it was engaged in government approved research; there is no other explicit exception for marijuana.

But the federal necessity defense is a creature of common law, frequently assumed if rarely cited by name, and Congress did not rejected it by name. Yet Congress did limit Schedule I to those controlled substances with "no currently accepted medical use," 21 U.S.C. 812(b)(l)(B). It assigned marijuana to Schedule I, 21 U.S.C. 812(c). Thus, "[i]t is clear from the text of the Act that Congress has made a determination that marijuana has no medical benefits worthy of an exception. The statute expressly contemplates that many drugs 'have a useful and

---

[3] *Kg., United States v. Duclos,* 214F.3d27, 33 (1st Cir. 2000); *United States v. Unser,* 165 F.3d 755,764 (10th Cir. 1999); *United States v. Milligan,* 17F.3d 177,181 (6th Cir. 1994).

[4] Justice Thomas wrote the opinion for the Court; Justice Stevens submitted a concurrence in which Justices Souter and Ginsburg joined; Justice Breyer took no part in consideration of the case.

[5] "As an initial matter we note that it is an open question whether federal courts ever have authority to recognize a necessity defense not provided by statute. . . .We need not decide, however, whether necessity can ever be a defense when the federal statute does not expressly provide for it. In this case, we need only recognize that a medical necessity exception for marijuana is at odds with the terms of the Controlled Substances Act. The statute, to be sure, does not explicitly abrogate the defense. But its provisions leave no doubt that the defense is unavailable," 532 U.S. at 490-91.

[6] "Lest the Court's narrow holding be lost in its broad dicta, let me restate it here:' [W] e hold that medical necessity is not a defense to *manufacturing* and *distributing* marijuana' *Ante,* at 494 (emphasis added).... Apart from its limited holding, the Court takes two unwarranted and unfortunate excursions that prevent me from joining its opinion. First, the Court reaches beyond its holding ... by suggesting that the defense of necessity is unavailable for anyone under the Controlled Substances Act. . . . [W]hether the defense might be available to a seriously ill patient for whom there is no alternative means of avoiding starvation or extraordinary suffering is a difficult issue that is not presented here.

"Second, the Court gratuitously casts doubt on 'whether necessity can ever be a defense' to *any* federal statute that does not explicitly provide for it, calling such a defense into question by a misleading reference to its existence as an 'open question.' By contrast our precedent has expressed no doubt about the viability of the common-law defense, even in the context of federal criminal statutes that do not provide for it in so many words. *See, e.g., United States v. Bailey"* 532 U.S. at 499-501 (Stevens, J., concurring in the judgement).

legitimate medical purpose and are necessary to maintain the health and general welfare of the American people,' §801 (a), but it includes no exception at all for any medical use of marijuana. Unwilling to view this omission as an accident, and unable in any event to override a legislative determination manifest in a statute, [the Court] reject[ed] the Cooperative's argument," 532 U. S. at 493.

The clarity of Congress' rejection of a medical necessary defense doomed the Coop's invocation of the constitutional avoidance doctrine, a canon of statutory construction available only in cases of ambiguity, *Id.*[7] The Court declined to consider the constitutional issues which might have called for avoidance in the face of an ambiguity because the lower court had not raised them, 532 U.S. at 493.

CONSTITUTIONAL ISSUES

Although the Court set them aside, the Coop's brief presented commerce clause, enactment clause and due process clause issues.[8] The commerce clause, in conjunction with the enactment or necessary and proper clause, empowers Congress to enact legislation regulating interstate and foreign commerce.[9] Congress passed the Act, at least in part, as an exercise of its powers under the common clause.[10]

---

[7] Under constitutional avoidance, "where a statute is susceptible of two constructions, by one of which grave and doubtful constitutional questions arise and by the other of which such questions are avoided, [the Court will] adopt the latter," *Jones v. United States,* 526 U.S. 227, 239 (1999).

[8] Brief for Respondents at 37-49, United States v. Oakland Cannabis Buyers' Cooperative, 532 U.S. 483 (2001) (No. 00-151) *(Brief).*

[9] U.S .Const. Art.I, §8, cls.3,18 ("The Congress shall have Power... To regulate Commerce with foreign Nations, and among the several States, and with the Indian Tribes . . . And To make all Laws which shall be necessary and proper for carrying into Execution the foregoing Powers and all other Powers vested by this Constitution in the Government of the United States, or in any Department or Officer thereof).

[10] 21 U.S.C. 801("The Congress makes the following findings and declarations ... (3) A major portion of the traffic in controlled substances flows through interstate and foreign commerce. Incidents of the traffic which are not an integral part of the interstate or foreign flow, such as manufacture, local distribution, and possession, nonetheless have a substantial and direct effect upon interstate commerce because - (A) after manufacture, many controlled substances are transported in interstate commerce, (B) controlled substances distributed locally usually have been transported in interstate commerce immediately before their distribution, and (C) controlled substances possessed commonly flow through interstate commerce immediately prior to such possession. (4) Local distribution and possession of controlled substances contribute to swelling the interstate traffic in such substances. (5) Controlled substances manufactured and distributed intrastate cannot be differentiated from controlled substances manufactured and distributed interstate. Thus, it is not feasible to distinguish, in terms of controls, between

COMMERCE CLAUSE

Congress' commerce clause powers are substantial but not unlimited. The Court summarized the scope of those powers in *Lopez* and *Morrison*, two instances where the commerce clause was found insufficient to support a claim of legislative authority. "First, Congress may regulate the use of the channels of interstate commerce. Second, Congress is empowered to regulate and protect the instrumentalities of interstate commerce, or persons or things in interstate commerce, even though the threat may come only from intrastate activities. Finally, Congress' commerce authority includes the power to regulate those activities having a substantial relation to interstate commerce, . . . *i.e.,* those activities that substantially affect interstate commerce," *United States v. Morrison,* 529 U.S. 598, 609 (2000), *quoting, United States v. Lopez,* 514 U.S. 549, 558-59 (1995) (internal citations omitted).

Recognizing that the boundaries of this last category of commerce clause power, intrastate activity with an interstate impact, are not always easily identified, *Morrison* and *Lopez* identified some of the signs which reveal that a regulated activity may in fact have no significant impact on interstate commerce. "First, we observed that §922(q) [the section at issue in *Lopez*] was a criminal statute that by its terms has nothing to do with commerce or any sort of economic enterprise, however broadly one might define those terms," 529 U.S. at 610. "The second consideration that we found important... was that the statute contained no express jurisdictional element which might limit its reach to a discrete set of firearms possessions that additionally have an explicit connection with or effect on interstate commerce," 529 U.S. at 611-12. "Third, we noted that neither

---

controlled substances manufactured and distributed interstate and controlled substances manufactured and distributed intrastate. (6) Federal control of the intrastate incidents of the traffic in controlled substances is essential to the effective control of the interstate incidents of such traffic...").

Other findings and declarations indicate Congress called upon its legislative powers to tax and spend for the general welfare of the United States, U.S.Const Art.I, §8, cl. 1, and to fulfill our obligations under treaties to which we are party, U.S.Const. Art.I, §8, cl. 18; Art.II, §2, cl.2: The Congress makes the following findings and declarations: "(1) Many of the drugs included within this subchapter have a useful and legitimate medical purpose and are necessary to maintain the health and general welfare of the American people. (2) The illegal importation, manufacture, distribution, and possession and improper use of controlled substances have a substantial and detrimental effect on the health and general welfare of the American people.... (7) The United States is a party to the Single Convention on Narcotic Drugs, 1961, and other international conventions designed to establish effective control over international and domestic traffic in controlled substances," 21 U.S.C. 801(1),(2),(7). The Single Convention obligates Parties to prohibit cultivation of marijuana in order to protect the public health and welfare and prevent the diversion into illicit channels, Art. 22, 18 U.S.T. 1408, 1419(1961).

§922(q) nor its legislative history contains express congressional findings regarding the effects upon interstate commerce of gun possession in a school zone," 529 U.S. at 612. "Finally, our decision in *Lopez* rested in part on the fact that the link between gun possession and a substantial effect on interstate commerce was attenuated," 529 U.S. at 612.

The Coop argued that "[o]nly the cultivation and distribution of cannabis in exchange for money or barter can be considered commerce, but even such commerce here is exclusively intrastate and therefore not within the power of Congress to regulate commerce among the states," *Brief at* 39.

Yet the Act, including its proscriptions on the cultivation, distribution and possession of marijuana, appears to be within the Congress' commerce clause powers as described in *Lopez* and *Morrison*. They identity as indicative of criminal statutes beyond the clause's reach those which purport to punish activities that have "nothing to do with commerce or any sort of economic enterprise." As the Coop's very name (Oakland Cannabis *Buyers'*) indicates, cultivation, distribution, or possession of marijuana almost always involves or is closely linked to some form of commercial activity - particularly if distribution requires the participation of physicians and health care insurers.

Moreover, while not necessarily dispositive by itself Congress' findings with respect to the interstate impact of the distribution and possession of controlled substances (including marijuana) provide further evidence that the Act does not exceed the authority granted by the commerce clause. Perhaps most telling of all, in response to challenges based on *Lopez,* the lower federal appellate courts have unanimously concluded that the Act is within Congress' legislative authority under the commerce clause.[11]

---

[11] *Eg., United States v. Edwards,* 98 F.3d 1364, 1369 (D.C.Cir. 1996); *United States v. Lerebours,* 87F.3d582, 584-85 (1st Or. *1996); Proyect v. United States,* 101 F.3d 11,13 (2d Cir. 1996)("the cultivation of marijuana for personal consumption most likely does substantially affect interstate commerce. This is so because it supplies a need of the man who grew it which would otherwise be reflected by purchases in the open market. As such, there is no doubt that Congress may properly have considered that marijuana consumed on the property where grown if wholly outside the scheme of regulation would have a substantial effect on interstate commerce"); *United States v. Orozco,* 98 F.3d 105, 106-107 (3d Cir. 1996); *United States v. Leshuk, 65 P3d UQ5,*1111-112 (4th Cir. 1995)("Leshuk contends that the Drug Act is unconstitutional because it regulates intrastate drug activities, such as the marijuana manufacture in this case, which do not substantially affect interstate commerce . . . . We ... reject Leshuk's Commerce Clause challenge to the constitutionality of the Drug Act"); *United States v. Dixon,* 132 F.3d 192,202 (5th Cir. 1997); *United States v. Tucker,* 90 F.3d 1135, 1139-141 (6th Cir. 1996); *United States v. Westbrook,* 125 F.3d 996,1008 (7th Cir. 1997); *United States v. Bell,* 90 F.3d 318, 321 (8th Cir. 1996); *United States v. Kirn, 94* F.3d 1247,1249 (9th Cir. 1996); *United States v. Wacker, 72* F.3d 1453,1475 (10th Cir. 1995); *United States v. Jackson,* HlF.3dl01, 101-102 (11th Cir. 1997).

Even if Congress lacks the legislative authority to ban cultivation, distribution and possession of marijuana under the commerce clause, its legislative authority to implement our various treaty obligations for the suppression of illicit controlled substances would probably be sufficient.[12]

ENACTMENT CLAUSE

When Congress enjoys legislative subject matter jurisdiction, such as the power to regulate interstate and foreign commerce, it may nevertheless elect to pass laws which exceed what is constitutionally "proper" under the implementary necessary and proper or enacting clause. For instance, legislation is not "proper for carrying into execution" constitutionally vested powers, such as those under the commerce clauses, when it seeks to "compel the states to enact or enforce a federal regulatory program" or to when it issues "directives requiring the states to address particular problems, [or] command[s] the states' officers, or those of their political subdivisions, to administer or enforce a federal regulatory program," *Printz v. United States,* 521 U.S. 898, 924, 934 (1997), *citing, New York v. United States,* 505 U.S. 144 (1992).

The Coop argued that Congress is not acting in the necessary and proper exercise of its legislative authority when it acts in total derogation of rights which the people of a given state have identified as fundamental unenumerated constitutional rights, *Brief at* 45-9.[13]

---

[12] Perhaps because the courts have rarely found it necessary to look beyond the commerce clause, the case law on alternative sources of legislative authority is sparse, but it does include *United States v. Rodriauez-Camacho,* 468 F.2d 1220,1222 (9th Cir. 1972)("Furthermore, the United States is a party to the Single Convention on Narcotic Drugs binding, *inter alia,* all signatories to control persons and enterprises engaged in the manufacture, trade and distribution of specified drugs. Marijuana (cannabis) is so specified. Enactment of sec. 841 (a)(1) is a permissible method by which Congress may effectuate the American obligation under the treaty").

[13] "This case represents an intersection of the Tenth and Ninth Amendments. The people have used the initiative power reserved to themselves under the Tenth Amendment to recognize a fundamental (sic) liberty interest they have retained under the Ninth Amendment. By an unwarranted extension of its powers under the Necessary and Proper Clause, the federal government now seeks to interfere with both the exercise of the power reserved by the people and the States and the rights retained by the people," *Brief at* 48-9.

"The Ninth and Tenth Amendments declare, "The enumeration in the Constitution, of certain rights, shall not be construed to deny or disparage others retained by the people," U.S.Const. Amend.IX; and "The powers not delegated to the United States by the Constitution, nor prohibited by it to the States, are reserved to the States respectively, or to the people,[51] U.S.Const. Amend. X.

The contention may have helped spur the three concurring members of the Court to urge at least a rule of construction that would recognize a medical necessity defense for marijuana possession.[14] The majority's sweeping dicta and the accompanying footnote which sparked Justice Stevens' comments, however, may reflect the fact that at least five members of the Court found the "necessary and proper" argument unpersuasive.[15]

DUE PROCESS CLAUSE

Of course, the Coop's Ninth Amendment fundamental-unenumerated-rights argument is closely akin to its substantive due process contentions, *i.e.,* that "these patients have a fundamental right to be free from government interdiction of their personal self-funded medical decision, in consultation with their physician, to alleviate their suffering through the only alternative available to them," *Brief* at 42-3.

The due process clause "provides heightened protection against government interference with certain fundamental rights and liberty interests. . . .[I]n addition to the specific freedoms protected by the Bill of Rights, the liberty specially protected by the due process clause includes the rights. . . to bodily integrity and

---

[14] "The overbroad language of the Court's opinion is especially unfortunate given the importance of sowing respect for the sovereign States that comprise our Federal Union. That respect imposes a duty on federal courts, whenever possible, to avoid or minimize conflict between federal and state law, particularly in situations in which the citizens of the State have chosen to serve as a laboratory in the trial of novel, social, and economic experiments. . . .By passing Proposition 215, California voters have decided that seriously ill patients and their primary caregivers should be exempt from prosecution under state laws for cultivating and possessing marijuana if the patent's physician recommends using the drug for treatment. This case does not call upon the Court to deprive *all* such patients of the benefit of the necessity defense to federal prosecution, when the case itself does not involve *any* such patients," 532 U.S. at 502 (Stevens, J. concurring in the judgment)(emphasis in the original).

[15] "Lest there be any confusion, we clarify that nothing in our analysis, or the statute, suggests that a distinction should be drawn between the prohibitions on manufacturing and distribution and the other prohibitions in the Controlled Substances Act [such as the prohibition on possession]. Furthermore, the very point of our holding is that there is no medical necessity exception to the prohibitions at issue, even when the patient is seriously ill and lacks alternative avenues for relief. Indeed, it is the Cooperative's argument that its patients are seriously ill, and lacking alternatives. We reject the argument that these factors warrant a medical necessity exception. ... Finally, we share Justice Stevens' concern for showing respect for the sovereign states that comprise our federal union. However, we are construing an Act of Congress, not drafting it. Because federal courts interpret, rather than author, the federal criminal code, we are not at liberty to rewrite it. Nor are we passing today on a constitutional question, such as whether the Controlled Substances Act exceeds Congress' power under the commerce clause," 532 U.S. at 494-94 n.7.

to abortion . . . [and in all likelihood] to refuse unwanted lifesaving medical treatment' *Washington v. Glucksberg,* 521 U.S. 702,719-20 (1997). The Court, however, has been reluctant to expand the concept of substantive due process, 521U. S. at 720, and has specifically refused to consider physician assisted suicide among the fundamental liberties so protected, 521 U.S. at 728.

Glucksberg seems to pose a major obstacle to recognition of a right to use marijuana for medicinal purposes, for it appears to have refused to acknowledge the right which the Coop claims. The Coop claims patients have "a fundamental right to be free from government interdiction of their personal self-funded medical decision, in consultation with their physician, to alleviate their suffering," *Brief* at 43. *Glucksberg* found that terminally ill patients facing the prospect of a painful death have no due process right to the assistance of their physicians to secure and assist in the administration of painless but fatal substances to alleviate their suffering.

Beyond this, the *Glucksberg* expansion tests are not particularly helpful. They require that those rights within the ambit of due process protection consist of "those fundamental rights and liberties which are, objectively, deeply rooted in this Nation's history and tradition, and implicit in the concept of order liberty, such that neither liberty nor justice would exist if they were sacrificed," 521 U.S. at 720-21. The history of the Coop's asserted right is arguable exactly the opposite. It is a history replete with government regulation of the practicy of medicine, of the distribution and use of medicinal products, of controlled substances, and of marijuana in particular.

Federal regulation of marijuana as a crime control measure dates back from the Marihuana Tax Act of 1937, 50 Stat. 551 (1937) by which time every state in the Union already regulated its sale.[16] The Act was modeled after the more general Harrison Narcotics Act of 1914 under which opium and other narcotics were regulated.[17] Congress passed the earlier Food and Drug Act of 1906 "to prevent the manufacture, sale or transportation of adulterated, misbranded or poisonous, or deleterious foods, drugs, medicines, or drugs and for regulating the traffic therein," 34 Stat. 768 (1906). In more general terms, "the practice of medicine ... has a long history of being regulated to protect the public safety."[18]

---

[16] Taxation of Marihuana: Hearing Before a Subcomm. of the Senate Comm. on Finance, 75th Cong., 1st Sess. 9-10 (1937)(testimony and chart accompanying the testimony of Clinton M. Hester, Assistant General Counsel, Department of the Treasury).

[17] H.R.Rep.No. 75-792, at 2 (1937); S.Rep.No. 75-900, at 3 (1937).

[18] *Pearsonv. McCaffrey,* 139F.Supp.2d 113,121 (D.C.Cir. 2001), quoting the observation from *Whalen v. Roe,* 429 U.S. 589, 603 n.30 (1977) that, "It is, of course, well-settled that the State has broad police powers in regulating the administration of drugs by health professionals."

Glucksberg's dicta seems to further undermine any contention that due process substantially restricts the federal government's authority to refuse to legalize marijuana for medical use. There, the Court cited *United States v. Rutherford,* 442 U.S. 544, 558 (1979), for the observation that "Congress could reasonably [determine] to protect the terminally ill, no less than other patients, from the vast range of self-styled panaceas that inventive minds can devise."[19] Here, Congress appears to have done just that. It has concluded that marijuana is highly addictive and has no accepted medical use, but permits reclassification of marijuana and its subsequent use when and if its medicinal benefits can be demonstrated under the procedures of the Controlled Substances Act.

FREE SPEECH

Finally, although the issue was not raised in *Oakland Cannabis Buyers' Cooperative,* the lower federal courts are divided over whether the First Amendment right to free speech shields physicians who prescribe or otherwise recommend marijuana to their patients. A court in the Northern District of California granted a preliminary injunction enjoining federal authorities from prosecuting physicians for such conduct. The order also prohibited federal authorities from revoking the physicians registration to prescribe controlled substances[20] and from excluding them from Medicare/Medicaid participation[21] for such conduct, *Conant v. McCaffrey,* 172 F.R.D. 681, 701 (N.D.Cal. 1997). The court subsequently made the injunction permanent in an unpublished opinion,

---

[19] *Rutherford* involved a patients' suit seeking to enjoin enforcement by the Food and Drug Administration (FDA) of restrictions on the use of Laetrile by terminally ill cancer patients. The court of appeals had affirmed the district court's injunction which directed the FDA to permit terminally ill cancer patients to use Laetrile, *Rutherford v. United States,* 582 F.2d 1234,1237 (1978), concluding that the Federal Food, Drug and Cosmetic Act, which required FDA approval of the safety and efficacy of new drugs, had no application to drugs intended for use by the terminally ill. The Supreme Court reversed. It could see nothing in the Food Act or its legislative history stating or implying that its provisions were limited to the drugs intended for use by the curably ill or that the drugs intended for the treatment of the incurably ill were exempted from the its demands. 442 U.S. at 552-57.

[20] In order to prescribe controlled substances, physicians must be registered with the Attorney General and their registration (DBA registration number) may be revoked on the basis of conduct "inconsistent with the public interest," 21 U.S.C. 824(a)(4), Federal authorities had indicated that they would consider providing, recommending, or prescribing marijuana conduct inconsistent with the public interest, 172 F.R.D. at 698.

[21] Individuals or entities may be excluded from participation based on "professional competence, professional performance, or financial integrity," 42 U.S.C. 1320a-7(b)(5). Federal authorities had likewise indicated that they would consider providing, recommending, or prescribing marijuana conduct sufficient for exclusion, 172 F.R.D. at 698.

2000 WL 1281175 (C97-001139 WHA)(N.D.Cal. Sept. 7,2000). It found serious questions as to whether the federal enforcement policy permitted a content-based restriction on speech and whether it was unconstitutionally vague, 172 F.R.D. at 694-98.

A court in the District of Columbia, on the other hand, refused to issue a similar injunction, *Pearson v. McCaffrey,* 139F.Supp.2d 113,125 (D.D.C. 2001). From the court's perspective, "there are no First Amendment protections for speech that is used as an integral part of conduct in violation of a valid criminal statute," 139 F.Supp.2d at 121. Therefore, "[e]ven though state law may allow for the prescription or recommendation of medicinal marijuana within its borders, to do so is still a violation of federal law. . . . The fact that speech or writing is the mechanism used by physicians to carry out such a task does not make the conduct less violation of federal law. The First Amendment does not prohibit the federal government from taking action against physicians whose prescription or recommendation of medicinal marijuana violates the [Act]," *Id.*

RELATED LEGISLATIVE ACTIVITY

State medical marijuana initiatives have provoked a mixed response in Congress including proposals to:

- require the Attorney General to revoke the controlled substance registration of any practitioner who recommended marijuana for medical purposes;[22]

- bar those who recommend marijuana for medical purposes from participating in Medicare and state health care programs;[23]

- clarify and increase the penalties applicable to Controlled Substance Act violations by registrants;[24]

- make mandatory, in those states with a medical marijuana exception, the discretionary denial of federal benefits for those convicted of controlled substance offenses;[25]

---

[22] H.R. 1310 (105th Cong.)(Rep.Solomon); S.40 (105th Cong.)(Sen.Faircloth).
[23] S.40 (105th Cong.)(Sen.Faircloth).
[24] S.40 (105th Cong.)(Sen.Faircloth).
[25] H.R. 1265 (105th Cong.)(Rep.Solomon).

- make it clear that Controlled Substance Act provisions continue to apply notwithstanding the massage of state medical marijuana laws;[26]

- provide that the Controlled Substance Act shall supersede any state law with which it differs;[27]

- study the impact of the California and Arizona medical marijuana initiatives;[28]

- create a federal medical marijuana exception to the Controlled Substances Act and the Federal Food, Drug and Cosmetic Act in the states with medical marijuana laws;[29]

- prohibit use of funds appropriated for the District of Columbia to conduct any ballot initiative to legalize or reduce the penalties for violations involving Schedule I controlled substances;[30] and

- prohibit use of funds appropriated for the District of Columbia to enact or implement any law to legalize or reduce the penalties for violations

---

[26] H.R3184 (105th Cong.)(Rep.Riggs).

[27] H.R.4802 (106th Cong.)(Rep.Souter).

[28] S.15 (105th Cong.)(Sen.Daschle); S.2484 (105th Cong.)(Sen.Leahy); S.9 (106th Cong.) (Sen.Daschle).

[29] H.R.1782 (105th Cong.)(Rep.Frank); H.R.912 (106th Cong.)(Rep.Frank).

[30] Pub.L.No. 105-277, 112 Stat 2681-150 (1998); *Turner v. District of Columbia Bd. of Elections and Ethics*, 77 F.Supp.2d 25 (D.D C. 1999) held that the provision did not bar the Board from counting, releasing, or certifying the results of the D.C. medical marijuana referendum.

involving Schedule I controlled substances (and prohibiting the D.C. medical marijuana referendum from taking effect).[31]

In the 107th Congress, Congressman Frank has renewed his proposal for federal compatibility with state medical marijuana laws under which neither the Act nor the Federal Food, Drug and Cosmetic Act would bar possession, prescription, dispensing or cultivating marijuana for medical purposes in those jurisdictions whose states laws permitted it.[32]

---

[31] Pub.L.No. 106-113, 113 Stat. 1530 (1999); Pub.L.No. 106-553, 114 Stat 2762A-34 (2000); PubX.No. 107-76, 115 Stat. 923 (2001). *Marijuana Policy Project v. District of Columbia Bd. of Elections and Ethics,* _ F.Supp.2d __, _ (D.D.C. Mar. 28, 2002) held that the provision regulated core political activity on the basis of content and thus its application to the plaintiffs was barred by the First Amendment.

[32] H.R. 1344 (107th Cong.)(also (a) instructing the National Institute of Drug Abuse to make marijuana available for an investigative new drug study, and (b) indicating the proposal is not intended to supersede laws which regulate smoking in public); H.R. 2592 (107th Cong.) (also indicating the proposal is not intended to supersede laws which regulate smoking in public).

INDEX